First Edition

CreateSpace Independent Publishing Platform

Dedication

I dedicate this book to my soul mate and wife, Marta Prosbova

Other Books by the Author

The Geographical Distribution of Animal Virus Diseases

Why I am a Happy Agnostic

1968 – My First Year in India with Johns Hopkins

TABLE OF CONTENTS

9

Prologue

I have decided to turn a liability into an asset and at the same time to kill two birds with one stone (so to speak). I am writing this in the city of Kosice in the east-central European country of Slovakia on 29 January 2009. It has been cold, cloudy and snowing for the past two weeks and the forecast on weather dot com predicts another ten days of snow and/or sleet.

I have absolutely nothing to do. Therefore, I want to turn this boredom into a useful stimulating project, i.e. write a book. During this endeavor I shall attempt to teach myself to touch type; hence, I will kill two birds with the one goal. I am in no hurry as I am retired.

This will be a journey of a life time, i.e. a journey of my life time as I remember it. I will record the significant experiences that occurred for each year that I have been alive (which I remember; or at least think I remember). Although, I think that it has been well documented that repressed memory, as well as old memories may be slightly erroneous or not true, I will make every effort to not distort any of the major facts. Also, since this is mainly a ploy to keep me occupied and to learn touch typing, I don't care if anybody else will be interested in what I write.

This really will not be an autobiography. I find them so boring. Who cares when and where you were at such and such a time. I am only going to tell anecdotes and short observations which I found significant. As the old Chinese adage goes, a journey of a thousand miles begins with a single step. So let's begin at the beginning.

BIRTH

I was told by those who ought to know (both of my parents, independently) that I was born 25 March 1937 [Europeans express dates as "25/03/37", while Americans express the same date as "3/25/37" - - - the European dating method is much more logical, i.e. day/month/year]. I had no womb-mate and escaped my fluid-filled confinement into the geographical location of San Diego, California. My father, who was a naval aviator, was ordered to help in the search for Amelia Earhart, the female aviatrix who was attempting to fly around the world and unexpectedly became missing. Therefore, my father was not in town when I was born. This may have been what angered my mother. Shortly after I was born she took me and my four year older brother, Charles, back to Oklahoma City, Oklahoma to live with her parents.

POTTY TRAINING

I remember my grandparent's house very well. There was a toilet downstairs under the staircase. On the toilet there was a yellow ducky potty seat for me to use. My grandparents had a part time black (in those days referred to politely as a negro, in Oklahoma) maid, whose name was Lola. I cannot say for sure, but when she first started to put me on the yellow ducky, I must have thought that she was going to flush me down the toilet and I would disappear forever, because my little legs would go into a running motion as she tried to get me to sit down and she usually had a very difficult time. Lola just laughed and was good natured about the whole problem. Actually, I liked the little ducky. It had a raised back and in the front where the duck's head raised up with sort of a splash shield so I would not pee on the duck's head or the floor.

It must have been comical to watch, as the process involved several unsuccessful attempts with Lola lifting me up and down several times before I would be settled onto the seat. She always wanted me to do "number two", i.e. defecate. If I did defecate she would say, "Good job". So later on when the routine was successfully established and I wanted to go to the toilet, I would eventually say, "Go jobbies", which meant I wanted to defecate.

HIGHCHAIR

Getting me into the high chair was a little like putting me on the yellow ducky. There would be several attempts to get my little legs between the tray and the seat back. But once settled in I must have been messy. The one time that stands out in my mind involved the dreaded word that has plagued me all of my life since then, i.e. RHUBARB. They tried to force a spoon full of rhubarb down my throat. Because of the feeder's obnoxious insistence, apparently I took my hand and pushed or shoved the small glass dish of rhubarb off of the tray on to the floor. This heinous act brought forth a severe reprimand, manifested by spanking the back of my hand with great gusto. It hurt and probably I cried. To this day, the word "rhubarb" sends chills up my spine and it is impossible to acquire a taste for this vile substance.

1938

BABY BED AND CROSS-DRESSING

I had to take naps in my baby bed. For a short period of time we had house guests from out of town. One of them was a little girl slightly older than me who quite appropriately wore a dress. My mother told me that shortly after I first saw her in a dress I would say that I wanted a "pant with one leg in it", meaning the dress. Of course, she refused to put me in a dress.

One day when I was supposed to be taking my nap, I crawled over the edge of my baby bed, went over to where the guest's clothing were and put on the "pant with one leg in it" and went back to the baby bed and went to sleep. When I woke up, I realized that I had peed and the girl's dress was wet. I then took off the dress and tried to hide it in the closet because I knew I had done something very bad. I do not recall the consequences or repercussions of this episode. However, I never tried cross-dressing again.

LOSING PLAYMATE

When my brother Charles first started to go to school, I had to be one year old. But I distinctly remember that day. Because for the first time in my life, my playmate was not around. My grandmother took me to the landing (the place where the stairs turned 180 degrees halfway between the first and second floors) and had me look out of the windows to a yellow building (the school) that I could see one block away. She told me that was where my brother was, but he would come back soon.

1939

HITTING PLAYMATE

I must have been about two or three years old and my brother therefore around six or seven years old. We were playing in the back yard after it had been raining and the ground of a flower bed was soft and moist. My brother took a play gun made out of tin and pushed it into the ground. He challenged me to pull it out of the mud. After struggling for a brief period of time, I was successful. He then rudely jerked the gun out of my hand and proceeded to push the gun back down into the moist mud very forcefully and then stated rather smugly, "There, I bet you can't get it out now."; "dummy" was certainly implied.

As I recall, it was not easy, but I struggled and struggled. It hurt my little pudgy fingers, but because of his taunting and superior air, I was determined. When finally I was successful, I took the gun and hit him over the head. Apparently, the end of the revolver was particularly sharp and suddenly, his blonde hair became bright red and blood poured out of the gash. He went running into the house crying.

An hour later, as I was still playing in the back yard, the door to the house opened and my brother with his head covered in white gauze like an Indian turban, came charging out of the door, probably intent on mayhem. Before he could reach me, my grandmother reached out and grabbed his arm and said, "He's just a little boy and didn't know what he was doing. He didn't mean to hurt you so". This apparently calmed him down and we are still friends to this day.

14

HOT IRON ON THE RUG

When I was four, my mother moved into a rented house across the street from a friend. I do not remember too much about it as we did not live there for very long. One day I found the iron and took the electrical cord and plugged it into the electrical receptacle.

Shortly thereafter, the smell of smoke enveloped the house and my mother came running into the room and pulled out the plug, but too late. There was a hole with the outline of the iron on the rug and the hard wood floor could be seen.

This reminds me of my granddaddy's favorite joke. He would ask me many times, "Why did the little moron burn a hole in the rug?"

Every time I would answer, "I don't know".

And he would reply with glee, "To see the floor show." He loved little moron jokes.

The other little moron joke that my granddaddy liked to tell me again and again was the one about the nightmares. He would say to me, "Do you know why the little moron took a bale of hay to bed with him every night?"

"No, granddaddy, I don't know."

He would reply, "To feed his night mares."

1941

WAR

When I was five years old, I had the job of collecting the newspapers from around the house and putting them into a golden covered box which was just the size of half folded newspapers. When the box was full, then the papers would be tied up and stored in the garage. One day when I picked up the Daily Oklahoman (the main newspaper), I folded it in half to put it into the box and noticed that there were just three letters filling up the entire top half of the front page. It said

"WAR". That was December 7th, 1941. I knew that something unusual had happened and my mother explained that war meant that we were going to have to fight another country.

1942

MY FIRST SCAR

There were tons of kids in our neighborhood. I was one of the youngest and smallest and when we played war games, I always had to be the dirty kraut (German) or Jap and thus, destined to lose. My big brother always had a higher rank than me also. One day we all had water pistols (squirt guns). I filled up a Mason fruit jar full of water for instant recharging of my water pistol. Carrying the jar in my left hand I charged into the fray confident in my abilities. However, I tripped on the curb and fell down on the concrete. There was water running next to the curb from someone who was watering their lawn. I remember noticing that the water was clear above my hand and broken glass and red after it flowed past my hand. As I recall (my first introduction into deductive reasoning) I was pleased that I had figured out that I must have cut my hand in the process. I never got stitches and I think that I licked it and tried to seal the fairly good sized flap of skin back into its original location.

1943

FIRST GRADE ACTIVITIES

In the first grade, I had one of the starring roles in a Whinny the Pooh play. I was Tigger the Tiger. It played before a packed house in the school auditorium. My brother went to the same grade school, but he was in the fifth grade. He distinguished himself to a much greater degree. There was a display case on the main floor of the school. Charles had made miniature Disney characters, like Mickey mouse, Donald duck, Goofy and others out of clay and had them playing instrument in an orchestral setting. Everybody was talking about it because it was so well done. I remember seeing it and being proud that he did it.

That evening we both told our mother and stepfather about it and begged them to go to the school and see it for themselves. So, after dinner we went down to the school and eagerly approached the display case. To our complete surprise, the heat of the lights in the cabinet had melted each of the carefully modeled characters into just lumps of unrecognizable clay. My brother was crestfallen. I was so disappointed also.

SANTA CLAUS; YEA OR NAY

There were two schools of thought amongst the elite of the kid's neighborhood playground. One school (the older kids) would say, "There is no Santa Claus". The other school (younger kids) said, "Yes there is." And then the arguments would follow; "Yes there is"; "No there isn't"; "Yes there is"; etc. This dialogue would go back and forth every year as Christmas would approach. Sometimes the debate would become so heated that the combatants would resort to profanity and taunting, such as; "Your father's moustache."; or "Yeah, well your mother wears bloomers."; or the worst insult of all, "Your grandmother's false teeth."

 Because of the high emotions raised my brother, who seemed to be a budding scientist, suggested that he and I could settle this argument on Christmas eve. My brother theorized that if there was such a thing as a true Santa Claus we could capture him when he came down our chimney. My brother's plan was for both of us to hide up on the second floor and wait until we heard a noise in the den where the fire place was. Upon hearing the expected noise, he and I would run down stairs with baseball bats and knock him out. My brother even had a rope that we would tie him up with before he could recover from our assault.

The plan never came to fruition, as we both fell asleep and woke up in our respective beds the next morning. We were embarrassed that we could not come to any conclusions from our botched well intended experiment.

1944

SECOND GRADE

In the second grade we moved to Hollywood, California and stayed in the Lido apartments on the corner of Yucca and Wilcox, one block north of Hollywood boulevard. There was a talent scout that lived at the same place and he wanted me to have a screen test for a role in the movie "Anna and the King of Siam". My grandmother was very

17

positive and I even memorized the lines. I still know them to this day. I was supposed to say, running onto the deck of a ship, "Mama, mama, are we there, are we there?" When my mother came back from a trip and found out about the screen test, she said absolutely no, in no uncertain terms. My grandmother and I were both disappointed, but I thank her for her foresight which kept me from being trapped in an artificial world.

1945

JAPANESE SURRENDER

We drove back to Oklahoma in July and stopped at the Last Frontier hotel in Las Vegas. I didn't know how to swim, but I enjoyed the swimming pool because it was so hot. I just held onto the side of the pool and went all the way around the pool semi-submerged in the water. Suddenly there was an announcement over the outside loud speaker and several people just jumped into the pool, some with their clothes on. I learned later that the Japanese had surrendered and the Pacific theater of the Second World War had ended.

In Hollywood, I attended an avant-garde modern progressive school that taught me absolutely nothing. All I did every day was to play cowboys and Indians and beat a big drum. At least, that's all I remember. The next year back in Oklahoma my neighbor talked me into going to his class on the first day of school even though he was one year older than me.

I will never forget my embarrassment. The teacher said, "And now class we will review our nines." I thought, what on earth was she talking about. Then in sequence, she would ask each student; "What is nine plus six?"; "What is nine plus eight?" etc. I had no idea what she was talking about. Of course, when she got to me, every time I had to say, "I don't know." So after class, she asked me to come up and talk to her. After she learned that I was a year younger than the other students, she sent me down to the third grade group. Because of the war, the third grade was split into a fast group and a slow group. You guessed it; I was sent to the slow group, because I had learned nothing in the second grade while in Hollywood.

ORIENTAL, OCCIDENTAL AND ORIENTATION

I did know how to look at a map and I did know east from west. When the teacher showed to the class on the big world map where the West Indies was, I thought to myself, 'How could the teacher be so dumb. It just could not be called the West Indies, because it is <u>East</u> of Oklahoma. It should be called the East Indies.'

Of course, much later I learned that since my native tongue is English and the English named everything relative to England; from their point of view, the West Indies was indeed west of England.

Just to fast forward (since I know I will forget it later), I had another epiphany in Calcutta relative to geographical reference points. I was walking down the main street of Calcutta (now called Kolkata) past the Air France ticket office. There behind the ticket counter was a world map that I thought was all wrong because they did not have the United States of America in the middle; France was. I had never seen a map before that did not have the US in the middle. It then dawned upon me that other people have a different frame of reference and of course, there is nothing wrong with that.

Rudyard Kipling wrote that, "East is east and west is west, and never the twain shall meet." However, I know that is wrong, because they both meet at the international date line in the middle of the pacific ocean; the 180th meridian.

1946

COLORADO TRIP

In the summer, my grandparents took me on a trip to Colorado in their car. My grandmother loved Rocky Ford cantaloupes. Every time we stopped to eat at a restaurant, I'd order hamburger steak. In Glenwood Springs, my grandfather deserted us and took the train back to Oklahoma City. When he got on the train, he told me to go around to the back of the train and wait. He walked back to the lounge car and appeared on the balcony at the very back of the train. When the train left, he flipped me a fifty cent piece.

FRUITS OF GAMBLING

During the same Colorado trip later on, at Steamboat Springs, my grandmother, Toots, her woman friend that accompanied us, and I went to a carnival. Toots was not her real name, which was Marie Mathews. They had a spinning wheel and there was a big crowd around it. As a little kid, I wormed my way in between the legs of the people standing and reached the front where they had a board with the numbers on it. There was one vacant space and I put the fifty cent piece down on that number. When they spun the wheel, it stopped on that number. Everyone was surprised that I had won. What did I win? - - - A pair of women's nylon hose. I went running to ask my grandmother what size hose did my mother wear. She told me and I went back to collect my prize. Later on, I felt bad because, I thought that my grandmother may have been hurt that I didn't get the hose for her. She never complained and I never brought up the subject. I have not been very interested in gambling ever since then.

1947

BIRTH OF MY LITTLE BROTHER
The big event of 1947 was the birth of my little brother on July 31st. After several months, I started to refer to him as the little turd. When an older person explained to me that the term meant a rounded piece of crap, I was embarrassed and stopped using the term immediately. I really have no idea where I picked up the word.

CHILD LABOR
I used to work after school while I was in the fifth grade. My uncle had a wholesale lumber business. Once or twice a week I would take the bus after school and do odd jobs like operate the mimeograph machine, stuff envelopes, operate the stamp franking machine, sweep out the office, etc. I think he paid me ten cents an hour.

HIT BY A CAR
On one trip to work, I got hit by a car. When the bus stopped, there were other people getting off behind me, so I had the bright idea of running in front of the bus and across the street, thinking that the cars behind the bus would be patiently waiting. To my utter surprise, I will never forget the flash of the blue rounded car fender that appeared out of nowhere. From an innate reflex I reached out and put my two hands onto the fender and pushed back as hard as I could. With the car's

slow speed and my reflex action, I went flying backward and did at least two summer-salts, up-righted myself and with the inertia, ran down the side street. The car turned the corner and drove along side of me and the lady driver said, "Are you hurt?" I answered, "No." Then she said, "Why didn't you watch where you were going you god damned dumb little son of a bitch. Don't you ever do something like that again."

NEWSPAPER BOY

I had a paper route throwing the "Advertiser" to the houses and apartments in about a twelve square block area. The clientele ranged from the very wealthy to the working class. It was a newspaper that I had to throw to every house and apartment and I never collected money from anyone at first. The Advertiser had about 15 to 20 separate paper routes divided into about 4 districts in Oklahoma City at that time. They had several contests for the "paper-boys". I wanted to win the first contest in my district which was selling subscriptions to the newspaper that everyone knew was going to be given to them whether or not they subscribed (which was a hard sell).

I worked real hard to win my district. One sales call I remember very well. It was in an apartment house on the second floor and the hallway was always dimly lit. A rough looking man in a sleeveless T-shirt answered the door and holler, "What do you want?"

I answered that I was there to collect for the "Advertiser".

He said, "What the hell is the Advertiser"?

I replied that it was the newspaper that I had to deliver to his apartment every Thursday and that it would cost ten cents a month.

He hollered, "I never asked for the damned thing. I never read it and it is so worthless that I only use it to wrap up the trash."

I looked up at him, disappointed that obviously I had lost a sale and said, "Well, at least if you wrap up the trash with it, it must have some use for you."

He looked at me like a light bulb had just been turned on and he said, "Hey, I guess you have a point there little man. How much did you say you wanted?" And I made the sale.

At the end of the contest, the winners were announced in the paper-boy information sheet which was delivered with the batch of newspapers dropped off at the paper-boy's homes. I wanted to win my district and sure enough, I won my district. When I went to show my mother of my achievement, she said, "What are you talking about? Turn the page over. Don't you see that you won the whole city?" I had not even bothered to unfold the information sheet, because I never expected that I would win the whole city and there at the top half of the page was my name as the overall winner. I went on to win the most yearly subscriptions sold and a year later I won the greatest increase in new subscriptions as well.

1948

SUMMER IN CALIFORNIA

In the springtime we took the train to California. On the way we went through Woodward, Oklahoma where they had suffered a devastating tornado. I remember looking out of the window of the train and seeing a scene that looked like that of London after the blitz from the rocket attacks by the Germans that I had seen in the newsreels in the movie theaters.

I lived with my grandparents at the Blackstone Hotel in Long Beach, California. Granddaddy would take me down to the Pike amusement park and watch me play different games. One morning as we sat down for breakfast my granddaddy said to my grandmother, "Ellen, Stewart and I are going back to Oklahoma City tomorrow." After a slight pause Mama Stewart said, "Barney, I wish you wouldn't." My granddaddy responded, "I'm not asking you. I'm telling you." ; and that was that.

Granddaddy had a big 540K Mercedes-Benz convertible. It looked just like the car that Hitler used to run around in that I saw in the newsreels at the cinema houses. My granddad loved that car and he used to love to race other cars. I remember one dark blue Buick

22

convertible that he raced along parts of route 66 highway in Arizona. He also liked to race trains when the tracks were paralleling the road.

FIRST DRIVING EXPERIENCE

One time in Arizona on a straight stretch, he asked if I wanted to drive the car. I said sure. So I sat in his lap and he operated the accelerator and the brake (if need be) and I steered the car along the two lane highway. The hood of the car was so long, it was difficult to see the road and keep the car on the right side of the road. Suddenly out of my peripheral vision, I noticed another car pulling up alongside of our car passing us. I said, "Granddaddy, granddaddy, take the wheel (meaning the steering wheel)."

He said, "No, you just keep on doing what you are doing. You are doing fine." The other car overtaking us was pulling an Air Stream trailer as well. While I was nervous, I knew that I had to concentrate and do a good job and everything turned out okay.

BUILDING CONFIDENCE

When we stopped in Flagstaff, Arizona at a motel, my grandfather gave me free rein to go play with some other little kids as much as I wanted and I really enjoyed myself playing with the other kids staying at the same motel. This was such a welcomed change from my mama (my grandmother) and mother who, bless their hearts, were so concerned for my welfare that they stifled any type of remotely dangerous activity. My granddad, conversely, allowed me much more freedom. I think that this contributed to a feeling of confidence in my ability to handle unusual situations.

DEATH OF MY GRANDDADDY

The most important and tragic episode in my young life was the death of my granddaddy. He had been ill with asthma and was hospitalized. My grandmother was staying at our house because it was much closer to the hospital. The telephone rang. I had always been taught not to answer the phone or listen in to other's conversations. However, something compelled me to pick up the phone downstairs and listen. I heard the doctor, Dr. Blue, tell my mama, "Mrs. Stewart, I have some bad news to tell you. Your husband has expired." I knew that photographic film could expire and that meant that it was not useful anymore and I put down the phone and cried immediately as I knew he had died.

POLICE EPISODE

My stepfather had a problem holding his liquor and thus everybody in the family had a problem as a result. One night our mother locked him out of the house when he was drunk. He was cursing and tried to break into the house by breaking the glass to unlock the door. My mother got frightened and called the police. My brother and I had baseball bats as the first line of defense and were waiting for him on the ground floor of the house.

When the police captured him and were holding him apparently he told them that this was his house and that there was no law to prevent a man from breaking into his own house. My mother was looking out of the second story window and one of the policemen said, "I'm sorry lady, this man is right. There is no way we can arrest him because there is no law against a man breaking into his own house." My mother responded that there must be something they could do, because she was afraid of him when he was drunk.

Our stepfather said, "See I told you dumb bastards there was nothing that you idiots could do."

Taking him roughly by the shirt, one of the policemen said, "Okay that's it. You are under arrest for insulting an officer of the law.", and proceeded to take him away.

The next day he called from one of the hotels downtown saying that he had known the night clerk at the city jail and had been released and threatened to jump out of the 26th story hotel window. When my mother told his "best friend" who was sitting next to her about this threat, his "best friend" grabbed the phone out of my mother's hand and said in a loud voice, "Do yourself a favor and everybody else and jump. Go ahead and jump", and then slammed the phone down. My stepfather did not jump.

1949

GOLF BALL LUNACY

24

My stepfather was an attorney who had big ideas. He had an office with a balcony in the APCO Tower office building downtown on the 32nd floor. At that time, he had few dollars and even less sense. One of our neighbors, Bill Coe, had an adopted son, Rocky, who was a year older than me. Under his influence we took two golf balls up to my step father's office. He wanted to throw the golf balls off of the balcony on to First Street. I said that such an idea was stupid and could hurt someone seriously. As a compromise, we walked down to the next floor and threw one of the golf balls out the hallway window so that it would hit Couch Drive, a much less busy street, one block north of first street. Boy did it bounce and no one was hurt. So, we threw the other golf ball.

We took the elevator down, retrieved the two golf balls and went back up to do it again. We threw the first golf ball out the window again and were about to throw the other one out the window, when the door to the stairwell opened and this man in a business suite came out and said, "I'm with the FBI and have been told that someone is throwing golf balls out the window of this floor. Do you boys have any idea who could be doing such a thing?" Rocky looked at me and I looked at him and both of us just shook slowly our heads. The man laughed and said that he really wasn't an FBI agent, but he was just casually looking out the window on the 32nd floor when he saw the golf ball being tossed out the window one floor down below. He said further that he could not believe his eyes and that we should not ever do such a thing again, explaining that it could kill someone if it landed on their head. So we never did it again.

1950

ESCAPE TO PHOENIX

One of my stepfather's other best friend was Clarence Black (also an alcoholic, as Oklahoma which was a dry state was littered with alcoholics in those days). Clarence's wife, Louise, had taken their two kids and left him. They moved to Phoenix, Arizona. My mother, who was also fed up with the constant tension and marital disharmony, used me and my asthma as an excuse to go to Phoenix. So, she took me out of Harding Junior High school, which I thoroughly enjoyed. In Phoenix, she enrolled me in a private school (Judson School for Boys) in Scottsdale, Arizona for the 8th grade. I loved it even better than Harding back in Oklahoma City.

EXPLORER SCOUTS EXPEDITION

The academics at the school were not that thrilling. The extracurricular activities were the most memorable. I learned to play tennis and really enjoyed the explorer scouts. Our troop flew down to Tucson to a Boy Scout jamboree in a C-47 transport plane. I wasn't worried at all, until they told us all to put on the parachutes.

One weekend we went on an overnight camping trip into the superstition mountain area. By the time that we finally reached the trail head near Tortilla Flats near Canyon Lake, it was almost dark. We struggled along the bottom of a canyon until we reached a complete blockage. So, we struggled and scrambled up the steep side of the canyon and totally exhausted, camped wherever we could find a small level spot. The next morning when we woke up, we could see that we were on the razor's edge separating two canyons and it was a miracle that no one fell off into one of the canyons.

SAVED BY THE FICKLE FINGER OF FATE

At the end of the school year my mother and I drove back to Oklahoma via the Salt River canyon. The road was under construction and there were sections where only one car at a time could pass. During one of these one way sections, right in front of us passed a huge bolder twice the size of a car. It went right in between us and the car ahead of us and missed us both. It was a rather sobering experience and an introduction into the frailties of life.

1951

SODA JERK JOB

When I came back to Oklahoma City, my mother had secured for me a job as a soda jerk in a drug store that was only about three blocks from our house. In order to train me how to make the various ice cream dishes and learn the ropes, I spent three full days at the carnation ice cream parlor retail store several miles away. The main thing that I learned was that we were supposed to refer to ourselves as, "soda dispensers", not "soda jerks".

During the training I screwed up on purpose several times under different tutors. For instance, I was told to make a chocolate sundae. So

26

I took chocolate ice cream and poured chocolate sauce all over it. My trainer said, "No, no, you should have used vanilla ice cream instead of chocolate. Make it again with vanilla ice cream."

"What should I do with the one I just made?"

"Throw it away." was his answer.

I countered in a surprised state, "Gosh, that would be a shame to just waste it. Could I eat it?"

"I guess so."

So, by making subtle errors every now and then, I got to eat lots of ice cream on the job.

After I completed my training, I said, "When do I get paid?" They informed me that the man that hired me would pay for the training. When I went to work at the drug store, the owner said that he never pays his prospective employees for the training period. So, I learned to never assume anything and always ask critical questions before embarking on new employment.

CUSHMAN MOTOR SCOOTER

I told my mother that I wanted to buy a motor scooter since I had reached the responsible age of 14 years old. She said that it was too dangerous and she would not allow it. However, I had my own money and theorized, that it was easier to ask forgiveness than permission, so I bought one anyway. She handled her fear in a nice manner and I had only one unfortunate accident.

I was riding my bright red Cushman motor scooter on a dirt road over to see my girlfriend. The road paralleled the fairway of the first hole of a golf course. There was a large pile of crushed rocks on the side of the road. The water sprinklers were directed on the fairway, but the wind was so strong that most of the water soaked the dirt road. I thought that the road may be mushy, but that if I speeded up, I could negotiate the wet road without any trouble. Unfortunately, when the front wheel hit the soft wet portion of the road, it started to wiggle back and forth and came to an abrupt halt, sending me flying over the handle bars. I landed head first in the crushed rock pile and literally had rocks in my head. My girlfriend dug out the rocks and cleaned up the bloody mess. To this day, my mother never found out about it.

SPIRITED ACTIVITY IN A NEW SCHOOL

In the Fall, I started a parochial school on the northern edge of the city called Casady School. Since I did not know anyone to begin with, as I was a new student, I studied and got really good grades. I liked sports and was fairly decent as a running back on the "tiny-tot" football team. After I got to know the kids, I guess one could say that I gravitated toward the troublemakers as opposed to the more academically oriented students. Then my grades declined and I sort of was more spirited than the decorum of the time demanded.

They had detention on Saturday morning from 9 am to 12 noon for kids who had received demerits and caused trouble and I began going to detention just about every Saturday. As I recall, you got 30 minutes for each demerit and I was there all morning long several weeks in a row at one stretch.

The school had a recess between 10:00 am and 10:15 am. They offered cookies and fruit drinks and sometimes some of the teachers would hang around and talk to the students. One time, one of the big tall teachers came up to me and said, "I want to talk with you." He asked me to follow him around the building away from everybody else. I remember thinking, 'this is really strange behavior. Why is he asking me to go where there isn't anyone around?'

When we got around to the other side of the building he said, "Is it true, what I heard about you; that you threw another student's shoe through a window and broke the glass?"

I answered respectfully, "Yes."

He said, "Why did you do that?"

I said, "Well first of all, I thought the window was open and some of us were just horsing around. I didn't do it on purpose."

Then he flattered me as he said, "What has happened to you? When you first came here, I thought to myself, here is the all-American boy. You were good in studies and good in sports and everyone liked to be around you. And now you seem to be in one scrape or another and your grades have gone down. I am so disappointed. How do you explain this?"

I looked up to him and said, "I guess I just got in with the wrong crowd."

I could see his eyes light up like a light bulb went off in his head. He smiled and said, "You hit the nail right on the head. What do you intend to do about it?"

I responded honestly, "I intend to stay in with the wrong crowd. They are a heck of a lot more fun than the other guys."

He didn't say another word, but just shook his head and wandered back around the corner of the building and disappeared.

I must say that I always respected and admired him because he was the only one that expressed a concern for my welfare. All of the other teachers just complained about my behavior and kept giving me demerits.

FOOTBALL INJURY

I remember thinking at the time of my last play of the game that if I cut back instead of making an end run, I might reach the goal line. Then, from out of nowhere Mickey Fentress came and hit me from the side and I went flying into the air. When I landed on the ground, all of my weight (what there was of it for such a skinny kid) hit the inside of my right knee. My patella (knee cap) was displaced out of its proper place to the lateral aspect of my knee joint. It is called a luxated patella or in slang, a dislocated knee.

The pain was excruciating. They put me onto a stretcher and took me to the nearest doctor. He tried manually to force the patella back into place which resulted in additional excruciating pain. Then they called an ambulance and they took me to the hospital which was many miles away. Unfortunately, there was a long section of the road that was under construction with many ruts and pot holes. Each bump on the uneven roadway caused even more pain.

I remember praying to God to stop the pain. Miraculously, the pain disappeared. I felt a tug at each bump, but no pain. I was exceedingly grateful to God to be so kind to answer my prayers and thanked him profusely. Years later, I learned that it is not unusual for people under extreme pain to concentrate on the relief of the pain so intently that they can actually cause the release of endorphins in their brain that causes the sensation of pain to be nullified. So, it wasn't God that did the miraculous act, but the will power of the brain.

When we finally reached the hospital and I was waiting in the ambulance for a gurney to wheel me into the hospital, a pretty young nurse came by. She stuck her head in the ambulance and said cheerfully, "My, what have we here?"

When they told her that I had dislocated my knee, she said, "Oh don't you worry. They will just remove the knee cap and you'll have a stiff leg for the rest of your life. But look on the bright side. At least you will not lose your leg." I have always been just a little bit skeptical of free professional opinions from well-meaning folks after that experience.

1952

FREIGHT YARD WORK

In the summer time I worked for my uncle at his lumber yard. My cousin, Barney (my uncle's son) also worked there. Our most difficult job was unloading box cars of lumber in the Oklahoma heat.

Once we broke the lock and opened the doors; one of us (we alternated) had to crawl up into the very narrow space between the top of the stack of lumber and the top of the boxcar. The lumber was wrapped by an approximately 6 inch band of tin to keep the lumber tight and prevent movement which might damage the lumber. We would take a large heavy tin snip and cut the tin band. However, there was always a problem to get the orientation of the cutting blades so that they would be at right angles to the tin to effectively cut the tin. If you did not have the blade surfaces at right angles, as the jaws closed, they just slid along the flat surface of the bands and did not cut it.

30

It was actually hard to breathe in the tiny space between the top of the lumber and the top of the boxcar it was so hot. So, you would try for a while and crawl back out of the boxcar to breathe momentarily and then go back in and try again to cut the tin strip.

But I must say, it was one of the best jobs I have ever had. You would work like a dog all day long. And it was strenuous work lifting very heavy stacks of shingles and moving bags of concrete mix, paint cans, etc. But when you got home, blew the black dust out of your nose and took a long cool shower, you felt great afterward.

YOU CAN'T TRUST EVERYBODY

At the lumber yard, there was a small store away from the main office near the truck entrance in the back of the main lot. They sold, paint, shingles and tools and other assorted items. It was called "Cash and Carry". One day as I was walking by, Chris, the foreman of the yard hollered out, "Hey, Stew come here for a minute."

"What's up Doc," I said mimicking the cartoon character Bugs Bunny.

"I gotta go up to the main office for a few minutes. Will you stay here and look after things? I'll be right back."

"Okay, but don't be gone too long because Barney and I have a load to bring in pretty soon."

After a short period of time, this nice looking young man came into the store. He "bought" some paint, some tools and then said to me, "Can I charge this stuff? I'm lower on cash than I thought."

"Gosh, I don't know. I've never done that before."

"Oh, it's real easy. I can show you how." he said. He showed me how to make out the sales slip and at the bottom of the slip he put: to be charged to: and wrote his name and address and telephone number.

Confident that I had now expanded part of my overall education, I beamed in my new found experiential enterprise as a super salesman.

31

After a while Chris returned and said, "How'd everything go old buddy?"

I said, "Great, I even learned how to make out a charge slip while you were gone."

"Charge slip? What are you talking about? We don't do any charging here in the cash and carry store. That's why it's called cash and carry."

It was a cruel lesson, but one of those experiences that you never forget and thus I benefited from it in the long run. However, the short run was rather humiliating.

A LONG LUNCH HOUR

The junior high school I had attended in Oklahoma City before I went to Phoenix had a sorority called the Happy Hearts. And even though I was now going to Casady high school, one of the prettiest girls in the Happy Hearts invited me as her date to the big sunrise social backward dance that they held once a year. The girls (who were too young to drive) had their mothers drive to the boy's houses and pick them up and took them to the dance which started around midnight (I think). Anyway, we would dance all night long, with breaks for refreshments and then enjoyed a sunrise breakfast. The mothers got the boys back to their houses around 5:30 or 6:00 am.

I was totally exhausted from dancing all night long and I knew that if I went to sleep for one hour, I would be incapable of waking up. So I successfully stayed awake for an hour and then rode my motor scooter to work in the freight yards at 7:00 am.

My uncle, who was the president of the company, had an air conditioned office with a big Naugahyde couch. The office had one door that opened into the air conditioned retail show room through which customers and sales people entered and it had another door which opened into the non-air conditioned back storage area.

My other cousin, Sharon (my uncle's daughter) operated the telephone switch board in the air conditioned retail show room (a cushy job that made Barney and I green with envy). At lunch time, I was totally exhausted and wanted to rest my weary bones somewhere out of the heat if possible to try and recuperate briefly over the lunch hour.

I asked Sharon where her Dad was. She said that he had gone to Wichita Falls, Texas on business, and he would be gone all day. In a stealthy move I went into the non-air conditioned storage area like I was going back to work in the yard and carefully opened the door to the president's office and looked around. Hooray! The air condition was on and the office was empty. So, I thought that I would just stretch out on the nice Naugahyde couch and rest for a few minutes before returning back to the freight yards.

The very next thing I remembered was that the door to the office opened from the retail side and a strange voice said, "Who is that?"

To which, I heard my uncle say in a matter of fact voice, "Oh, that's my no good lazy nephew." Then directing his comments to me he said, "Stewart, what are you doing here?"

I replied, trying at the same time to brush all of the sawdust and dirt off of his Naugahyde couch, "Oh, I'm just taking a little snooze on my lunch hour."

"Lunch hour", he exclaimed. "It's 7:30 pm."

To his credit, he didn't fire me, not only because I was his sister's son, but because he probably paid me a lot less than someone else. Also, I explained to him the logistics of the Happy Heart sunrise social backward dance, although he didn't seem to be very sympathetic to that as an excuse for my somnolent behavior.

ESCAPE TO RHODE ISLAND
While my drunken stepfather was beating up a drunken Indian in a motel in Colorado, my older brother, Charles, brought up an enticing proposal. He asked if I would like to accompany him to go and see our real biological father in Rhode Island. I said that that was a rhetorical question. Our mother was slated to call us from her "vacation" in Colorado that evening and we could ask her if I could go also.

The phone call followed an anticipated pattern: No, I could not go to Rhode Island because I had asthma and needed to be near doctors. She further explained, "I don't care that you are working in the freight yards. You are frail and you can't go."

Then, the great decider came on the phone trying to sound sober. "No. no.", my stepfather said. He also stated that if I insisted on going, that Charles could not go. Sooo, we said, "Okay", hung up the phone and then we left for Rhode Island.

Since theoretically, we stole the family car, Charles thought that the highway patrol would be looking for us. Therefore, we took the back roads instead of the major highways. We reached St. Louis around midnight and got lost wandering around the big industrial areas which were scary. After we finally left St. Louis and were on our way I went to sleep. When I woke up, we were on a dirt road and it was pitch black outside. Charles was asleep in the front seat. I shook him and said, "What's happening? Where are we and what are we doing here"?

He responded that he was very tired and had to rest. Even though I was only 15, I suggested that I drive for a while, because I didn't like sitting out in the open in a totally unknown area. He said that would be okay and he got into the back seat and went to sleep. I turned on to the major highway and drove and drove until I saw a sign that said, "St. Louis 15 miles". Then a little light bulb turned on inside my brain and I realized immediately that I had turned onto the highway in the wrong direction. Charles never knew.

MEET FRATERNAL GRANDPARENTS

When we got to Baltimore, I felt like we were in a foreign country. I had never seen row houses before. We learned from neighbors that our dad's parents had gone to Atlantic City, New Jersey for a vacation. We found them at the Clarion Hotel on the boardwalk. To say that my grandmother was overbearing would be an understatement. As we walked along the boardwalk our grandfather, Purtsie, would say, "I think that the boys would like to - - - - -". My grandmother would interrupt, "No, the boys wouldn't like that." I thought to myself, 'Why isn't someone asking the boys?'

When we finally arrived in Fort Adams in Newport, Rhode Island and my father opened the back door of the car where I was asleep, I didn't know what to call him. I could have said, "Hi dad"; "Hello father", "How ya doin' pop". So as a compromise, I said, "Hi, Captain."

INTRODUCTION TO CATHOLICISM
My dad's second wife, Peggy McCormack, was Catholic and therefore my father adopted Catholicism. They went to mass every Sunday. So, without any previews of coming attractions, my brother and I accompanied the whole family (which included four little girls, 2,4,6 and 9 years old) to church that first Sunday.

As we walked through the door of the church, I noticed that people stopped and put their hand in a bowl of water and let some dribble onto their forehead, so I did the same. We sat down in a pew. All of a sudden everybody stood up, so I stood up. As I looked around, everybody had sat down again and I was the only one standing up. So, I sat down and all of a sudden everybody stood up again. So, I stood up again. And again, suddenly I was the only one standing up. So I sat down.

I had trouble understanding what was being said by the priest and the congregation. At first I thought they were saying things like, 'I can play dominos better than you can', or 'eat some spirit candy.' Then it dawned upon me that everybody was not mumbling, but speaking Latin. The whole sermon was in Latin, which was Greek to me, or Farsi, or Zulu. At any rate, I was one lost soul and didn't like it. I told my dad afterward, that I'd rather play tennis while they went to church and he said, okay.

MAKE UP YOUR OWN MIND
Toward the end of the summer my grandmother came back from Europe on a ship and Charles and I drove to New York City to pick her up. We drove back to Newport where she stayed in a hotel while we were going to pack and then drive her back to Oklahoma City. Then Charles and I would drive back to Newport as neither of us liked our stepfather. The night before we were to leave, my brother and dad got me in the den, sat me down and proceeded to tell me that I should not drive back with Mama Stewart because if I did go back to Oklahoma City, I would more than likely stay there.

I argued that I loved to travel and I was sure that I would come back. At one point either my brother or my father said, "You are growing up and it is time for you to make up your own mind and you should stay here."

"I have made up my own mind. I want to go." I responded.

They said that I just thought that was what I wanted to do and they were both adamant that I should stay there. So I acquiesced and let Charles drive back Mama Stewart and then he drove back by himself. He then started going to the Rhode Island School of Design in Providence and I started Rogers high school in Newport.

DOMESTIC VIOLENCE
One of the reasons that I did not relish the idea of returning to Oklahoma City was because of the shenanigans of my alcoholic stepfather. Little did I realize at the time that I was going from the frying pan into the fire. My stepmother turned out to be an alcoholic also.

Peggy had been a very successful singer with a blind piano player named George Schearing, and was a budding actress in England when she met my father and married him. She was very active in acting in plays in Newport. One night after the end of one of the plays in which she performed, she got completely drunk at the cast party.

Apparently, my dad and she got into some sort of an argument. All I remember was some sort of a scream that woke me up and very shortly afterward Peggy was standing in the doorway to my bedroom screaming, "See what a wonderful father you have. He just knocked my front teeth out."

She turned on the light and opened her mouth to show me her missing teeth. There was blood all around her mouth and some dripping off of her chin. After her brief announcement, she turned on her heels and walked into their bedroom. My father came into the room and explained that she was drunk and had threatened to take the girls out into the night and away. He said, he had no other choice but to hit her when she wouldn't listen to him. His hand was bleeding and portions of the skin from his first interphalangeal joints to his knuckles were missing from two fingers and the bones were exposed.

I asked if he was all right, did he think that Peggy had settled down, and would they be okay. He said that he thought so and he went into the bedroom and shut the door. No sound came out of the bed room, so I assumed that everything was okay.

The next morning at breakfast, even with a hangover, they both were discussing the next step. They both agreed to concoct a story to tell the respective medical authorities about some fictitious accidents that had caused the traumas. My dad said that he would say that he tripped and fell on a porcelain vase and cut his hand. My stepmother said that she would say that she tripped and fell on one of the iron fire place devices and knocked her teeth out.

What amazed me was that they both just decided to lie and everything seemed to go back to normal. They were, of course, worried about the consequences of pressing criminal charges with the subsequent investigation and involvement of the police.

My dad wore a bandage around his whole hand for a week or so and Peggy got two new capped teeth from the dentist and that was that.

UNLUCKY AT LOVE

The first girl I ever kissed was Dolly Lamb in Oklahoma City. I asked her to go steady with me and gave her my Indian serpent ring. She said that she didn't want to hurt Grey Fredrickson's feelings as he was also courting her at the same time. So she wore my ring around her neck on a chain and we were hot and heavy at times.

She went away to a summer camp and wrote me very nice letters. Then I left Oklahoma City to go meet my father and decided not to return to Oklahoma City. I felt bad about deserting her, but she still wrote very nice letters to me and asked me to come back to Oklahoma City. When I was dating her, she said that "Blue Moon" would be our song. I didn't care that much, but if she cared so much, I thought, okay, "Blue Moon" will be "our song".

My brother Charles and I took the train back to Oklahoma City during our Christmas vacation and Dolly asked me to go to the school Christmas dance which was at the top of the First National bank building in downtown Oklahoma City. I was in a good mood and happy to be with Dolly. The band began to play the song "Blue Moon" and I romantically asked Dolly, "Do you want to dance?"

She answered, "No. That's Grey's and my song." I never asked her to dance again.

WHEELIN' AND DEALIN'

My brother Charles came back to Oklahoma for the summer. Since I had turned 16 years old, he said that I needed a car instead of a motor scooter. To that end we drove around town looking for a small car for me. I remember we drove a little light green Morris-Minor and took it over to our great-grandmother's house to show her and Charles lobbied her to buy it for me. I remember thinking that it was so nice of Charles to do that and he was so considerate of my welfare.

The next thing I knew was that out of nowhere Charles had a very spiffy, bright blue MG –TC open roadster and was leaving for Rhode Island. As he packed up to go back, he said, to soften the blow that he had a new vehicle and I only had a motor scooter, "By the way, I am giving you my old 1941 Plymouth."

Filled with gratitude I responded, "Thanks. But where is it?"

"Oh, its downtown at the repair shop getting a new motor put in. All you have to do is go down there and tell them that I gave it to you and it is yours." he said.

So, he left for Rhode Island and I got one of my buddies to drive me downtown to get Charles's old 1941 Plymouth with the new motor installed. I told them at the shop that I was there to pick up Charles Odend'hal's car and they brought out the car. I got in and started to drive out of the shop, but the owner came running up to me and said, "Hey, where do you think that you are going?"

I said, "Home. This is Charles Odend'hal's car isn't it?"

38

In an emphatic manner he said, "It's not Charles Odend'hal's car until you give me $113.78 for the REBUILT motor I just installed."

My mind quickly recalled that Charles had tried to sell his car for $350 to the husband of our black maid, who came to clean our house once a week. I had the $113.78 in the bank from working all summer. Therefore, I calculated rapidly that I might be able to make a nifty profit. So I paid for the car.

Ten minutes later as my buddy, Bernie Hodge (who was following me back home) approached a curve in the road, his ability to see the road was obscured by black smoke. The smoke emanated from my newly acquired '41 Plymouth that had stopped running and was convalescing on the side of the road. With a rope, Bernie towed the '41 Plymouth back downtown to the shop. They agreed to fix it.

The next week, again I went down to pick up the car. Because of the smoking episode, I thought, I will turn the purchase of the '41 Plymouth into a quick profit. So, I drove the car into the first used car lot I came to on the way home.

A salesman in a bright gaudy multicolored sport jacket walked up to me as I got out of the car and said, "Can I help you?"

Not beating around the bush, I blurted out, "How much will you give me for this car?"

He walked around the car fairly rapidly and said, "How does $45 sound?"

With an unconcealed shocked expression on my face I said, "Gosh, I just paid $113.78 to have a new rebuilt engine put in this car."

His response will ring in my ears forever. He said very slowly, putting his sympathetic hand on my shoulder, "Son, that was your mistake; not mine."

BUYING THE MODEL A

One day while driving across the North Canadian River bridge on May Avenue near the stock yards, I saw this blue model A Ford with a for sale sign on it on the side of the road right next to the bridge. I pulled over and walked over to the car. A man came out from under the bridge and asked if I want to buy it. When he offered to sell it for only $75, I said, yes I would take it.

I didn't even drive it. I just asked if it ran okay and he answered in the affirmative. I asked him for a receipt and he said to follow him. He went down under the big cantilever bridge to his house which is hard to describe. It was a combination of several apple crates stacked together, with asphalt like tarpaulins draped over the sides. Inside the dirt floor living space, there were several electrical devises, like a fan, what looked like a refrigerator and a radio. There was also a proper bed and some cabinets. He gave me a receipt. When I went outside I noticed a long electrical cord leaving the top of this shack which on the ground which eventually disappeared.

DRIVING THE MODEL A

The model A was a 1929 model, but the hood was from a 1931 model B and did not fit properly, so I could not latch it down and it sort of flapped up and down, like it was trying to fly, if I went too fast. I was reluctant to drive fast anyway because the mechanical brakes didn't work very well. As I would approach an intersection, many times, I had to rub the right front wheel into the curb to stop the car. Sometimes, I even had to resort to opening the front door and drag my shoes on the street surface to help stop the car.

Out of idle curiosity, I wanted to know how fast the car would go. So, I asked one of my friends (Charles Walbert) to follow me in his soup up Dodge and let me know the top speed, since I did not have a speedometer. As the model A approached the top speed, suddenly the hood just flew off of the car and flapped on over to the side of the road. The oil breather cap blew off and oil came leaking up through the floor boards drenching me and my white shirt in oil. It even got on the wind shield and I had to stop, as I could not see. The model A survived this extreme exercise and I retrieved the hood and put it back on. No adverse effects resulted. My friend said that it had reached a top speed of 67 miles per hour.

ELUDING THE POLICE IN THE MODEL A

One fringe benefit of having an alcoholic stepfather around the house was that there were lots of "siphon" bottles around. These were seltzer bottles with a spout on the top and a handle to release the soda water for mixing alcoholic drinks. A new bottle could propel the soda for quite some distance (about 5 or 6 feet).

In the summer time, there were several locations where lovers would go to park their car and neck and pet and mess around. They would leave the windows open because it was so hot. The model A sat so high up, it was really easy to sneak up alongside of the loving couple with the lights off, stop next to their car and my buddy (Bernie) would spray them with the soda from the siphon bottle and we would take off before most of them could chase us.

One fateful night around 11:30 pm, Bernie and I drove around the back of the barn that functioned as our gym at our high school. Sure enough, Bill Leney and I think, Cathy Mulvey were necking in his car (a recently acquired speedy Chevrolet coupe) and they were stretched out in the front seat with the windows down. As we slowly coasted by without any lights, Bernie gave them a healthy blast of soda. Well, Bill Leney was the captain of the football team, two years older than us and much much bigger and stronger. So I gunned the motor and left the area in a cloud of dust. However, I saw his head lights come on and I didn't want to wait around to see where he might be headed.

I drove into the nearby residential section and rapidly changed directions trying to lose Bill. In my haste, I ran through a stop sign on one of the major streets. The major street had no shoulders of significance and a half a block away, a police car pulled onto the road crosswise to block my model A. Remember I had mechanical brakes with poor stopping power. So, as I approached the police car, I knew that I could not stop in time and my only available option was to go off of the road onto the very steep sloping roadside and go around him, hoping that I wouldn't tip over because the model A had a very high center of gravity. I still hit the brakes, but nothing much happened. As we went gliding past the police car with his spot light trained directly on my face, the policemen hollered out, "You ran that stop sign."

Looking directly at the spot light I said, as I passed by, "I know it."

The way he had blocked the road, I knew it would take him a minute or so to go back and forth to chase me, so I gunned it and turned down the first street I came to. About a half of a block down that street I saw a house on the left with a big car parked in a double car driveway, with just enough room for me to stop next to it, so it would shield my car from his view. Unfortunately, under emergency conditions and the fact that I had one mad football player and one mad cop after me, in the heat of the moment, I had forgotten about the defective mechanical brakes. So when I tried to stop pulling into the drive way, nothing happened and the model A slammed into the garage door of this house. Immediately, lights went on inside the house. As the cop car went speeding down the road past the house, I backed out of the driveway and headed back in the opposite direction.

Neither the football player nor the cop caught me. However, as luck would have it, two days later I had another run in with the same cop. The suburb where our school was located was a very small community and the policemen had to do double duty. After school, I had at least 6 other buddies of mine in the model A. They were on the running board and in the rumble seat at the back. The cop was directing the little kids across the street from the elementary school. He was stopping traffic and when he saw my very distinctive car (I had painted a very bright red stripe on the side). He walked up to my window and said, "You were the ornery brat that ran that stop sign over there last Wednesday; weren't you?"

When confronted with over whelming incriminating evidence, I resorted to my only logical defense; i.e. I lied. "No, it couldn't have been me because I was sick last Wednesday and missed school. You can ask my mother."

"Don't you lie to me. I recognized this car with the big red stripe on the side." he retorted.

"Oh.", I replied, "Tommy Smith has a car just like mine with a big red stripe and he lives in this area too."

As the traffic was backing up while this conversation was going on, he said, "Okay, you can go on your way this time. But I'll be looking after you my young man and if you so much as look cross eyed, I'll run you in. So be careful from now on."

1953

DON'T EVER LIE TO YOUR GRANDMOTHER

In desperation, my mother divorced my alcoholic stepfather and left town. She went to Dallas, Texas and I went to live with my grandmother. All of my cousins and my brother called her mama Stewart, but I just called her mama, because that's what my mother called her and I always called her the same name.

Like most of my pals, I started smoking cigarettes when I was in the 10th grade. After living with my grandmother about a year and a half, she posed a question to me. She said, "Stewart, you're not smoking cigarettes are you?"

"Nope mama," I replied, casually lying.

A few weeks went by and again mama asked me the same question and I gave her the same answer.

Another few weeks went by and again she asked me if I was smoking, as she had seen a number of young kids my age smoking.

At this constant questioning I became angry. "Gosh darn it mama, you keep asking me the same question and I'm getting tired of it. Do you think that I would lie to my own grandmother? Quit bugging me about it and leave me alone."

Mama was quiet for a minute. The silence bothered me and I thought, maybe I was too severe with her and she could not take the shock of me barking back at her. Then she said, "You know Stewart, you will be going away to college one of these days and perhaps it might be important to you to be able to wash your own white shirts."

Now I thought, she's flipped out and she doesn't even know what she's doing. I decided to humor her and do as she suggested, when she asked me to follow her into the kitchen.

On the kitchen counter were my white shirts, underwear, T-shirts, socks, etc. Patiently standing behind her trying to conceal my boredom, my mama said, "Noticed that the first thing you do, is to empty all of the loose tobacco out of the shirt pockets."

Stunned at this unexpected revelation, I stammered, "Oh, mama, I have been carrying Bernie Hodge's cigarettes around for him because he doesn't want his mother to know that he is smoking."

She just looked at me in the eyes and sympathetically stated the coup de grace, "Stewart, you have been carrying Bernie Hodge's cigarettes around for him since before he even moved to Oklahoma City."

"Haaa, ha. You got me mama. You are absolutely right. I apologize. I have been lying to you and I am sorry. I will never lie to you again. I promise." And thus endeth the first lesson.

1954

DRIVING MOTHER TO DALLAS

My mother had moved to Dallas. One time I drove my mother and little brother down to Dallas from Oklahoma City. Shortly after we crossed the Red River Bridge that separates Oklahoma from Texas there was a four lane highway. The two lanes headed north was a newly completed concrete highway that was smooth and level. The two lanes headed south was the old highway that was not level or smooth, but had many hills and also had many dips in the road.

Shortly after entering Texas, my mother said that she wanted to take a short snooze. She climbed into the back seat and Leonard, Jr, took her seat in the shotgun position in the front. After a while, a Studebaker came screaming by us driving like a bat out of hell. My little brother said, "You're not going to let him do that to you are you?"

As my manhood had been challenged, I put the pedal to the metal and we began to roar down the dippy highway. At one point, I figured that when we had almost caught up with the Studebaker, we had hit over 100 miles per hour. Then suddenly, we hit a dip so deep that we were air borne at the other side of it. I instinctively looked in the rear view mirror to see if my mother had been awakened. To my surprise, all I saw was my mother levitated horizontally blocking the view out the back window.

To say, she was not happy, would be a vast understatement. She was livid, I was livid at Leonard, and Leonard was livid at the Studebaker.

THE FAKE BOMB INCIDENT

Here is the evolution of this high impact project. Barney, my cousin had been making firecrackers and lighting them in his back yard. Some of the neighbors had apparently complained about this activity to the police. In discussions about this, I think I suggested as a joke of making a fake bomb and rolling it into the little police station building in Nichols Hills. Nichols Hills was to Oklahoma City what Beverly Hills was to Los Angeles.

The Nichols Hills police station was just one room with one door. When you opened the door it lead into a short hallway ending in this very small room where there was only room for a couple of desks. Off of the hallway, there were storage cabinets on either side. The idea was (stupid), to open the door and roll a fake bomb into the room and see if the cops would jump out of the windows which had no screens. It was a pretty dumb plan as I look back on it some 50 or so years later. But you have to remember that I was a trick loving teenager with a strong hormonal soup coursing through my blood at the time.

I picked out an empty potassium permanganate rounded cardboard container from the trash at school. I asked our chemistry teacher if he thought that powered charcoal was rapidly combustible (explosive). He said something to the effect that it was not rapidly oxidizable. With that meager assurance, we decided to go ahead with the project.

Barney and I together assembled the fake "bomb". We filled the bottom third of the container with BBs, pored melted candle wax to cover the BBs and then filled the remainder of the container with powered charcoal. Later on, we added black masking tape all over the 6 inch cylindrical container and stuck in a 30 second dynamite fuse that we bought at a construction supply house. It did look formidable.

We were not too worried about the cops because we had terrorized them before and escaped their clutches. We basically thought that they were pretty stupid. We had done all kinds of pranks on Halloween and not been caught. As a matter of fact on the night of the project, I drove out to Nichols Hills to pick up one of our accomplices, Charles Schweinle, III.

There was this little kid about 5 or 6 years old wandering around Schweinle's immediate neighborhood. No one knew who he was, so Charles and I took him to the police station. We brought him inside the police station and told the officers that we had found this little lost boy. Their response astounded me. They said something to the effect that; yes, they had received a call from a distressed mother that her son of about that age was missing. Unfortunately, they did not bother to get her name, address or phone number. However, they took the little boy and said that the lady was bound to call back before too long.

After leaving the police station, we drove back into the city and picked up one of my other buddies, Jay Bernstein. All three of us were attending a rapid reading course at the medical school on the east side of town. After the course, we drove by my uncle's house and with a secret call, Barney snuck out of the house and we were on our way.

When we drove by the police station about 11:00 pm, to our surprise there was no one in the building. We theorized that they must have been next door in the fire station playing cards or something like that. Therefore, Barney and I took the fake bomb and waited in the bushes on the side of the building and Schweinle and Bernstein would go to the gas station across the street and call the police. Then we expected that the cops hearing the phone from next door would come back to answer the phone. When they walked through the door, we would toss the fake bomb through the window and watch them scurry. However, the phone rang and rang and no one came.

So plan B was for Charles and Jay to operate the getaway car and Barney and I would toss the fake bomb into the fire station just for fun. We had 15 minutes to meet the getaway car on a back street. Barney held the fake bomb and I tried to light it, but the wind was so strong, I had a great deal of trouble. Barney said to let him try to light it and he handed me the fake bomb. After a while the fuse was lit and burning. I looked at it in my hand and thinking it isn't supposed to go off, but I think I will get rid of it as fast as I can. So I decided to toss it through

46

one of the upstairs windows and we ran to the designated meeting place.

A few minutes later we brazenly drove by the police and fire stations. We saw several flash lights outside underneath the broken window and some of the investigators were pushing the potassium permanganate container with a broom or a mop handle. They held up a trash can lid for protection. Boy did we laugh and we thought that we had escaped Scott free. Little did we ever anticipate the rapidly approaching future resultant unexpected development.

Unfortunately, when Barney tried to sneak back into his house, his father caught him and asked him, "Where have you been?"

Barney responded, thinking fast on his feet, "I went on a Phi Lambda hay rack ride with kids from Classen high school."

To which my uncle said, "Who did you go with?"

Barney said, "Stewart Odend'hal, Charles Schweinle and Jay Bernstein."

At that very moment, the doorbell rang, even though it was well after midnight.

Barney offered to get the door, since he was down stairs and his father was at the top of the stairs. When Barney opened the door, two stern looking uniformed police officers were there. One of them asked, "What have you been doing tonight Barney to have fun?"

Before Barney could answer, the other officer said, "That's not black dynamite powder you have all over your hands is it?"

At that point, my uncle said, "I don't care what he did. He did it. Just take him away. And you can go and pick up Charles Schweinle, Jay Bernstein and, Stewart Odend'hal. I'll give you the addresses and phone numbers."

All I knew, as this was occurring, was that we had chalked up another successful prank that resulted in another embarrassment for the

Nichols Hills police. Smiling to myself, I carefully eased my grandmother's Cadillac along the driveway and into the garage without any lights. I tiptoed up the stairs of our duplex with my shoes off and thought that I had successfully reached my bedroom without being detected. As soon as I quietly closed the door to my bedroom, the telephone rang. I heard my grandmother say something to the effect, "Yes, I understand. I'll tell him." And then she hung up the phone.

Quick as greased lightning, I jumped into bed with all of my clothes on and pulled the covers up to my neck and proceeded to fake an angelic expression on my face which was all to no avail. My grandmother opened the door, switched on the light immediately and stated (even though I had my eyes closed), "You needn't bother to get undressed. I don't know what you've been doing, but the Oklahoma City police are coming by to pick you up. Please wait downstairs. I'm going back to sleep."

I felt pretty stupid lying in bed with all of my clothes on. I remember thinking, "Oklahoma City police? They must have me mixed up with someone else." Within about 15 minutes the police car stopped in front and I got into the back seat as they indicated. To my surprise, guess who was already in the back seat; my buddy, Jay Bernstein. They took us out to the police station in Nichols Hills.

We were interrogated, finger printed and threatened to be sent to the boy's reformatory in String Town, Oklahoma. Only one of the parents came down to the police station and that was Mr. Schweinle. He offered to pay for the window and asked that we be released. After about 2 or 3 hours of questioning and intimidation, they let us go and drove us back to our respective houses.

Charles Schweinle said that when the cops came to pick him up, his mother was crying and said, "Charles, Charles, after all of the money that we spent on you and you turned out to be a juvenile delinquent."

The incident was on the front pages of the newspapers and on all of the radio and TV reports. One of the reports stated, that "With this latest arrest of the perpetrators of the bombing of the fire station, the crime statistics should drop in the city."

We had to divert the attention of my 92 year old great-grandmother, so she wouldn't see the 5 o'clock news and perhaps suffer a heart attack. There were lots of aftershocks, too numerous to mention. Ironically, Jay and I were our school safety representatives to an all-state meeting with school safety officials who came to Oklahoma City from Washington D.C.

During the meeting, Jay wanted to ask the guy from Washington D.C. what he thought was going to happen to the boys that threw the fake bomb into the fire station. I said for him not to do it, but he did it anyway. The man said that he suspected that all of the boys were from wealthy families and that nothing much would probably happen to them.

Years later I was finger printed and investigated by the FBI, so that I could join and fly for the Civil Air Patrol in New Mexico. So, I suffered no adverse effects from that teenage indiscretion that I know of.

1955

THE COTTON BOWL CAPER
Our high school basketball and soccer teams went to Dallas, Texas to participate in a tournament. My mother had moved to Dallas a few months before. So one night I borrowed her car (silly mother) and a couple of my buddies and I cruised around the town. We bought some beer (of course) and saw the sights.

Around midnight we drove into the Texas state fairgrounds where the cotton bowl stadium is located. The entire area appeared to be completely deserted. There were several broad streets separated by broad green medians. Roaring around one corner, apparently I drove through a stop sign. Schweinle said, "Hey, you just ran that stop sign."

Playing the fool (as usual), I slammed on the brakes and came to a screeching halt (way past the stop sign) and told my law abiding buddy that this abrupt stop would make up for the one that I just missed.

Before I finished the sentence, a spot light hit me right in my eyes, as there was this cop car parked across the median from where I had just slammed on the brakes. As soon as I realized that it was a cop car, I

49

floored the accelerator and we took off. The chase was on. I would elude them and they would reappear. Often, we would end up again going in the opposite direction on these median streets which had very high curbs. This repeating pattern of seeing and not seeing the cop car continued for about 20 minutes. It must have looked something like the keystone cop movies of olden days.

At one point, I saw this ramp that went up alongside of the cotton bowl and drove up there with my lights off. The ramp leveled off for a short distance around the midfield position and we stopped the car and waited for the cop car to pass. We waited and waited and then because of the beer, we could wait no longer for anything. We hung our penises over the small ledge and all three of us enjoyed a mighty micturition.

We could hear the urine hit the pavement down below and then all of a sudden we heard a different sound. Well, like urine hitting some sort of tin object. We all looked at each other, leaned over the ledge and lo and behold there was the cop car slowly moving without its lights turned on.

"Ah, ha", I said. The cops had been hot on our trail and they knew the direction we were going around and around the cotton bowl. They knew that we were the source of the pee that pounded their car. And therefore, they knew that we had to come down the ramp in the same direction they were headed. So they stopped right behind the junction of the ramp leading downward and the street they were on.

Therefore, I didn't start the car motor, but I took off the hand brake and we pushed the car backward until it rolled down the ascending ramp. When we reached the bottom, it was quite some distance from where the cops were waiting for us at the end of the descending ramp. We started the car and took off in the opposite direction and we never saw them again.

I am so lucky that I am alive. Later on that same night, we drove over to where they were building the new Amond Carter Fort Worth airport. At that time, only a few of the buildings were completed, but the runways appeared to be finished. So, I drove out on the runway and floored the accelerator and I think we hit 105 miles per hour. My mother (bless her heart) never knew about any of this stuff.

I just recalled an amusing incident on the way down to Dallas on the bus. Rob Rainey was asleep with his head back and his mouth wide open. One of our teammates could not resist the opportunity. He took out his foamy shaving cream dispenser, aimed the pointed end directly into Rob's mouth and filled up his oral cavity with the shaving cream. After gagging and coughing, Rob spewed the stuff all over the person sitting in front of him. Lucky, no harm was done and Rob never suffered from inhalation pneumonia.

MIAMI BEACH SCAM

My mother came back from Europe by ship and landed in Nassau off the coast of Florida. She suggested that a friend and I drive down to pick her up in Miami. So Robert Shirley and I drove from Oklahoma City to Miami. We were driving a 4 door 1953 light blue Mercury. We arrived in Miami after midnight and immediately got lost.

There were very few cars on the road. At a stop light, this car with two young couples pulled up alongside and the driver asked if we were from Oklahoma. I answered yes. He said that if we did not have a place to stay the night to follow him. I said, okay and proceeded to follow him for a while and then suddenly I turned off and left them. Robert said, "Why did you do that?"

I said, "We don't know those guys from Adam and I just don't trust 'em". I was proud of my decision and thought to myself smugly that this is one Okie hick that will not be taken in by nefarious characters. Unfortunately I had been a little premature in my self-congratulation.

The next evening we drove to Miami Beach to see the big hotels and walk around. All of the parking places on the streets were taken, so I pulled into this dimly lit parking lot. As I started to step out of the car, this man came up to my door and said, "You can't park here. This is the Savoy hotel parking lot."

I said, "I don't see any signs that say that."

He said, "Look at the side of that building." Pointing to a large sign, it clearly said, "Savoy Parking Lot".

I responded sheepishly, "Oh, gosh, I didn't see it. I can hardly read it from here since it is not lit."

He then said, "Okay that'll be $10 for parking here illegally."

I returned, "I didn't park here. You told me not to and I haven't even gotten out of the car."

He then stated quite authoritatively, "Give me $10 or I'll call the police."

I looked him in the eye and I said, "Go ahead. I'll be more than happy to wait right here."

He countered, "Okay. I think I'll let you off this time."

I just rolled up the window, started the motor and drove out.

Later on we found a parking spot on one of the side streets. As we were walking down the sidewalk of Collins Avenue, we saw that on the sidewalk there were these large cut out figures where you could stick your head in a hole. The photographer would take a picture of you as Donald duck, Mickey mouse, or a pirate. I asked how much and was told $5.00. So Robert and I did it. After he took the picture, I asked when we could come back to pick up the pictures. He said, "In a couple of days."

I responded that we were leaving the next day. He said, "Give me your address and I'll mail them to you." You guessed it; we never got anything in the mail. So, I have always been suspicious of anything to do with Miami.

ACCEPTANCE TO THE UNIVERSITY OF THE SOUTH
Throughout my life, I have delighted to volunteer at cocktail parties that I graduated 20th in my high school class. After the congratulatory comments which usually followed, I would add that there were only 24 in my graduating class. It always got a laugh (the alcohol helped).

The summer between high school and college, I had resigned myself to the fact that I would go to Oklahoma A & M (A & M means Agriculture and Mechanical) College at Stillwater, Oklahoma. I decided to do this because many of my friends were going to go to Oklahoma University (OU) in Norman, Oklahoma. They were mostly from very wealthy families and it didn't matter what they studied, they had money behind them and they would do okay regardless of their academic prowess or lack thereof.

My dad was a naval officer and was not wealthy. I knew that if I went to OU, I could not resist a good time and I probably would not study much. I thought I'd better go where I didn't know anyone and therefore I would study and do better and learn more. Besides, I had already been rejected by Stanford, Pomona and UCLA and my other choices were slim to none.

I was working at W & W Steel Company; digging ditches, operating drill presses, automatic screwing machines, welding, etc. Toward the end of the summer, Jerry Jordan called me and said, "Hey Stew, why don't you come with me to Las Vegas?"

I replied, "Gosh, Jerry, I can't afford to go to Las Vegas."

Jerry said (and I'll never forget this), "Stew, you don't understand. You can't afford not to do this. My Dad just bought the Riviera Hotel and it won't cost us anything."

I was dumb founded. Without a second thought I said, "You sweet talking silver tongued devil, since you put it that way; of course I'll come with you to Las Vegas." So we drove out there the week before school was supposed to start.

Once there, I took my hard earned money and would play black jack and hang around the slot machines (like I was playing) and got all of the free mixed drinks I could hold. The hotel rooms had these really dark thick drapes and when they were closed, you couldn't tell whether it was light or dark outside.

One day (possibly night) the phone rang in our room and woke me up. I had no idea whether it was light or dark outside, much less what day of the week it was.

A familiar voice said, "Stew, whatcha doin?"

I responded sleepily, "Trying to get some sleep you jerk. You woke me up."

My friend Pat McHenry then said, "How'd you like to go to Sewanee?"

I said, "Are you talking about, the river that Al Jolson sang about?"

"No dumb ass. I'm talking about the place where the University of the South is."

"I never heard of it. Why on earth would I ever want to go there."

Pat said, "Schweinle's going there."

"Gosh, sure I'll go there then. Can you get me in?"

"No problem. I have already investigated and I can get you in for sure."

"When are we supposed to be there?"

"Three days from now, so you'll have come back right away."

"Jeez, Mac thanks a lot. Are you absolutely sure that I can gain admission?"

Pat said, "I'm absolutely sure. A piece of cake my friend."

"Okay. I'll go. I'm on my way."

Pat said, "Great, I'll make all of the arrangements. See you in a couple of days."

As I started to say goodbye and hang up, a passing thought shot through my mind and I blurted out, "Hey, wait a minute, I don't even know what state it's in. Where is it?"

"Tennessee." was his response.

1956

PARTY WEEKENDS

Sewanee was an all-boys school in those days. If I had known that at the time, I probably would not have wanted to go there. However, there were nine fraternities on the "mountain" (as the University of the South was called). Just about every weekend, one of them would have a party and that meant girls.

Since nobody lived in fraternity houses and everybody lived in dormitories, you had lots of friends who belonged to different fraternities. Therefore, when there was a party at one of the fraternities, it was okay to drop by and see what was happening.

At any rate, Page Faulk and I lived in one room and we shared a bathroom with the guy next door who lived by himself. I can't even remember his name, but let's call him Butch for short. Butch had been on a toot and had locked our door to the bathroom that we shared and then passed out on his bed in his pajamas.

When I could not get into the bathroom, it sort of pissed me off. I risked my life by climbing out of our window on the second floor. I could just barely reach the fire escape landing. From there it was easy to climb inside of the open window of the bathroom. I looked at Butch and it was obvious that he was dead to the world.

This was at about 11:30 am that Sunday morning. Page and I hatched a plan. We with the help of other accomplices picked up Butch's mattress so that he was like a wiener in a mattress bun and carried him outside for about two blocks and put him down on the ground in front of the heavily attended main church. With the birds singing and in bright sun shine, people streamed out of the church at 12:00 noon and saw Butch snoring away.

Shortly after the doors opened one of the professors shook Butch to awake him up. He sat up, rubbed his eyes, looked around and calmly gathered up his blankets, bed sheets and then lifted the mattress over his head and walked back to his dorm.

ON TO CALIFORNIA

My mother wanted to move to California and also to visit my brother and his wife who were due to have a baby. I was 19 years old, my little brother, Leonard Jr. was 9 years old and my mother was 42 years old. We piled into my mother's 1955 Chevrolet Capri and we took off for California. Two incidences stand out in my mind. One involved getting a ticket by the highway patrol in Colorado and the other when we checked into a motel in Nevada.

I was driving across the flat eastern part of Colorado. Suddenly I realized that I was going 90 miles per hour. I said, "Gosh, I'm going over 90 and I didn't realize it." Leonard was hanging over the back of the front seat and duly noted my statement. I slowed down. The usual posted speed limit was 60 mph. Before I knew it, my speed had crept up to 70 mph. As I approached a row of trees on either side of the road, I remember distinctly thinking that I should slow back down to 60 mph.

Then from out of nowhere in the rear view mirror I saw a highway patrol car right behind me with the flashing red and blue lights. So I pulled over and waited for the highway patrolman to come up to our car window.

He said, "Do you know how fast you were driving?"

I answered, "Yes sir, I was going 60 miles per hour."

He volunteered, "Didn't you see the 50 mile per hour speed limit sign back there?"

I responded truthfully, "Gosh no, I didn't see it."

As he took out his ticket writing tablet, suddenly my little brother blurted out, "You should have seen him back there when he was going 90 miles per hours."

The officer looked up as I smiled sheepishly and I said, "That's my little brother for you. He has a really good sense of humor."

I had my right elbow resting on the back of the seat between my mother and me. Leonard's face was just behind my elbow and for a fleeting second I had the urge to bop him in the mouth real hard with my elbow. But I didn't.

The second incident involved checking into a motel somewhere in Nevada. When we stopped at the motel, somehow we got into a conversation with a man in the parking lot. I do not recall what the topics were, but it lasted a few minutes. Then my mother went inside to check in with the office. After she had excused herself, the man we had been talking to asked me, "Have you and your wife travel far today?"

This shocked and amused me. I explained that she was my mother and he was suddenly shocked and amused. My mother was glowing when I told her later about the exchange.

TRANSCONTINENTAL BRUSH WITH CAR TROUBLE

In the summer of 1956 I spent working at various jobs in Los Angeles, California, living with my mother and little brother in Altadena, which is just north of Pasadena. I bought a 1954 black Mercury coupe with fender skirts from one of my work mates at the filling station.

In August I drove back to the University of the South. On the way I experienced a little car trouble driving through New Mexico. I stopped in Tularosa, just north of Alamogordo because my radio went out and I couldn't figure out why; neither could a mechanic at a filling station. So I continued on without a radio.

On the way to Roswell, the two lane road was very narrow without any shoulders and a straight drop off on each side of the road. The road was just a series of one hill after another. The road would climb for a while and then descend for a while before repeating this pattern for mile after mile. Both the ascending and descending segments were quite steep and sometimes (mainly) short.

Maybe 20 or 30 miles west of Roswell I started losing power as I went up the hills. A line of cars accumulated behind me. What began as a slight loss of power developed into a very strange situation. My car would gain speed going down the hills, but would lose power going up the hills. The loss of power evolved into gradually diminishing speed going up the hill until the speedometer hit 26 miles per hour, then power would return and briefly the car would speed up until it passed 26 mph again. So it would lurch forward for a second or two and then go slower.

There was no place at all to turn off of the road and the accumulation of cars following me became quite long. In some places the hills were so close together that no one could pass me. Some of the drivers behind, in utter frustration, did pass me dangerously going down the short hill segments. I was so embarrassed. As folks would pass me they looked at me like I was an idiot and I certainly felt like one.

I will never forget my relief when I saw Roswell miles away and the road was all downhill. I pulled into the first filling station I came to, even though the sign said "closed". I went to the back of the station and knocked on the door of the house immediately behind. A mechanic who lived in the house agreed to help me even though it was Sunday evening about 7 pm.

He checked everything and said that the problem was the generator. He put new brushes in and charged up the battery. I started the car and I noticed that the amp meter indicator needle was flipping back and forth wildly. The mechanic said that happens until the new brushes wear in and gradually that would stop.

It was about 11 pm by that time, but I thought I will soldier on. Around 2:30 am the radio went out. About 15 or 20 minutes later, I started to lose power going up even very slight rises in the road. Then as I was nearing Hereford, Texas, the head lights started to flicker and go dim and then brighten and then go dim again. The lights went so dim that I worried that oncoming cars might not be able to see me. So I pulled off of the road and slept near some roadside vendor.

When I woke up the next morning and was thankful that it was a Monday, I drove straight to the local Ford-Mercury dealership. I explained the problem and walked around town while the service folks tried to discover the problem. When I got back, they said that they had figured out the problem and that it was the generator. I said that I just had new brushes put in the night before and that it couldn't be the generator. They said that it must be the armature of the generator and that they would replace it and everything ought to be okay.

Intrigued by this unusual development, I finally decided to investigate the affected regions under the hood to see what I could find out. I didn't want to spend any more money than necessary. They had jacked up the front end of the Mercury. I crawled underneath and looked around. Eureka! I saw where the coated wire running from the generator to the battery was missing its insulating cover and the naked wire was hitting part of the iron frame under the radiator.

I respectfully declined their offer to "fix" the generator, bought some friction tape, wrapped up the wire, had the battery charged and was on my way. The take home message from this experience was that when things go wrong, don't count on others, be they experts or well-meaning friends; do your own investigation first in a thorough manner.

Now the 26 mph lurching and dying of the power can be explained by the fact that the Mercury had an over drive that kicked in at 26 mph. There was not enough juice (voltage) in the battery to activate the overdrive. The least essential electrical items closed down first, so the reverse hierarchy was the radio – overdrive – lights – spark plugs.

Many years later, I learned during my veterinary training that you look for the most simple explanation first and then proceed to the more complicated possible causes of a malady before making a diagnosis. In other words, when presented with a limping animal, start with the bottom of the foot, looking for a thorn and then go up the leg gradually checking for other explanations.

1957

UCLA

At the University of the South, I rarely studied hard or with a great deal of diligence. I made A's, B's and C's during my two year career there. I did enjoy myself and liked the professors. It was a very comfortable place in many regards. Someone cooked your food, did your dishes, washed and ironed your clothes, made your bed and cleaned your room. There was another pleasant opportunity for student-teacher interaction. I believe it was every Wednesday evening, all of the professors had to remain in their houses between 6 and 8 pm. They were open to having the students drop by and visit with them about anything. I think I did it only once with my biology professor. However, it was really a nice idea.

In the summer of 1957 I lived with my mother and little brother in Pasadena and again worked at odd jobs. I visited the University of California at Los Angeles (UCLA) and was impressed with the physical plant and the different courses that they offered compared with Sewanee. So I applied to transfer in the fall.

A week before school started I received a message to see one of the admission officers. He introduced me to an attorney who was to establish whether or not I was a legitimate in-state student or if I should be classified as an out of state student. He informed me that in order to be admitted as an in-state student, I would have to provide him with a copy of the divorce papers that stipulated that my mother had sole custody of me, since I was living with her in California.

I casually mentioned that my father was in the Navy and he lived in a house in Alameda, California. He said, "Oh, no problem then. You are an in-state student." I was happy that I did not have to pay out of state tuition for sure. All UCLA cost was $62 per semester. It was referred to as an activity fee, since they said it was tuition free.

Since I was on the campus, I thought that I would attend the orientation presentation for the freshman. I had the impression that UCLA was just another big state university and that it was like the University of Oklahoma, where if you had a high school diploma, that was all that you needed to go to OU. I didn't think there would be a particularly competitive atmosphere.

Much to my surprise, I had a rude awakening. The speaker at the orientation session said, "Most of you probably did very well in high school. However, this does not mean that you will do well here. I must point out to you that only about 10% of the high school graduates in the state of California are accepted to UCLA. So you are going to have to work harder than you did in high school to survive here."

My second rude awakening was when I visited my assigned faculty advisor. I waited in the hall outside of his office until he called me to come in. I had just sat down in front of his desk when a colleague opened the door and said, "Hey, how about going over with me to the cafeteria and have a cup of coffee?"

My advisor said, "Okay, as soon as I get rid of this kid here."

It was obvious to me that I was of secondary importance. It seemed to me throughout my career at UCLA that the students were just a nuisance and a distraction to most of the professors. They had the attitude that teaching was a good profession, if it wasn't for the students. Research and publish or perish were their major concerns.

The third rude awakening was signing up for courses. Several people told me to get to the sign-up tables early, because there was just limited space in each course since most of the regularly attending students had already signed up by mail. Okay, I thought, I'll get there right at 8 am when they open up for course selections.

To my consternation, the first course sign-up table I went to had maybe a 50 to 70 students waiting in line to sign-up for that one course. By the time that I finally did sign-up, when I went to the other tables, all of the courses that I wanted to take were already full. Bewildered, I decided that I would take the courses offered to the Physic and Chemistry majors and not the watered down courses I wanted to take for the non-majors.

My take home message from this experience was to pay more close attention to advice relative to punctuality in the future. Ever since then I have always been early to most every appointment, be it business or pleasure. But in a way, I have to thank the experience at UCLA for the message that absolutely no one cares about you. It made me realize that if I was going to do anything, I had to rely on my own efforts and not expect anyone to help me out.

When I got my first semester's grades I was overjoyed. I had, following very concentrated studying, received a C grade in everything, even though I had dropped two courses. Until I got my grades, I was fearful that I would receive a D in everything. UCLA was not difficult, but the caliber of the students made it difficult because everyone else studied so hard.

The next semester, I was determined to do better and I really burned the midnight oil. I had a 4.0 (all A's) at midsemester and my grades were not a problem from then on. However, I did go to my physics professor and tried to get him to give me a B grade. I got a B on every test that he gave, but he gave me an A for my official midterm grade. I asked him if he didn't make a mistake. He said that he did not make a mistake because he graded on a curve. Only 10 % of the class got an A. I said, but I got a B an every exam. He said that since I got a high B on every exam, others may have received a low A on one exam and then a low C on the next and when everything was averaged out, I was in the overall A range. I told him that if he didn't give me a B midterm grade, and insisted on the A, it would destroy my incentive to get a 4.0. He said, he had never ever had a student come in and insist on receiving a lower grade and he would not change it.

SPUTNIK

I got most of my meals free as I worked as a "hasher", i.e. waiter, mainly for breakfast, sometimes for lunch, but always for dinner. I prepared the tables, served the meals, and then cleaned up afterward for the Acacia fraternity. Everyone was talking about the satellite that the Russians had launched on October 4th of 1957. When we had finished cleaning up the dishes around 7:30 pm, we all gathered out in front of the fraternity house and looked westward. Sure enough, as predicted, there appeared a fast moving star like light that came zooming from west to east. The sputnik only was visible for less than a minute, but had a tremendous impact on my imagination. We all figured that it was only a matter of time before a human would be a pioneer in space.

USC SABOTAGE

UCLA's biggest rival was the University of Southern California (USC). That fall we played football against them in the Los Angeles Coliseum. It was going to give us a chance to show off our card section where several hundred students would form different signs and messages by holding up big square colored placards. I think that the game was going to be televised as well.

I was sitting in the tenth row from the bottom. I confidently took out the card that told me what colored card to hold up for the different displays. The director speaking on the microphone said to take out the cards for display number one. I prepared the green card and then he said, "Up." We all held up our different colored cards.

The director looked and could not believe what he saw, so he rapidly said, "Down, down." We all complied.

Then he said to take out the colored coded card for the second display and said, "Up." Again, he rapidly reversed himself and told everyone in a screaming voice, "Down, down."

He then explained that every display was not what was intended. Instead of saying messages like, "UCLA triumphs", or "Go trounce the Trojans (USC).", what he saw was the opposite signs, like, "UCLA are wimps", or "USC over UCLA".

What apparently happened was that the committee responsible for the preparation of the codes was infiltrated by USC students, who switched all of the card directions to show USC favorable messages. I have to give the USC perpetrators credit. I admired their masterful deception. However, it was very embarrassing to UCLA.

Luckily, I usually brought along with me to the football games oranges, in which I had injected vodka by a hypodermic syringe and needle. So, I was not as upset as some of the other non-drinkers were.

1958

A QUESTION OF REFERENCES:
My second semester I took a course in parasitology. I had to write two term papers; one before the midterm grade and one before the final. The first paper I wrote was on amoebiasis. When my report was

returned, on the front page of my paper, I could make out a B+ and a C+, that had been written in pencil and then erased and in black ink a distinctive D- was clearly evident.

Confused and disappointed, I went several times to talk to the professor. When I finally found him in his office, I asked him about my grade.

He responded, "Oh, I don't know anything about your term paper grade. That's handled by the reader."

"The *reader*?" I stammered.

"I'm much too busy to read all of the student's reports. I hire a reader to read them and give them a grade."

"Where can I find the reader? I have some questions to ask." I cautiously enquired.

"Go see Miss Jones. She works at the medical center in the physiology department. Now if you don't mind, I have a lot of work to do and it doesn't include you."

So after several unsuccessful trips down to the medical center, I finally met Miss Jones. When I asked about my paper, she said that she thought it was a good paper and that she had learned something from it. She added that she had put the B+ on the front, however when she looked at the meager 8 references in the bibliography, she had erased it and put the C+ on the paper. She said that she did not put the D- on the paper. That must have been put there by the professor.

So, with paper in hand again I made several trips back to the professor's office to ask him about this turn of events. I finally caught up with him and asked him if he was the one who put the D- on my paper.

He looked at it a little more closely than before, tossed it back to me and said with an air of contempt, "Yes, I remember now. I gave you a D- because of you didn't have many papers cited in your reference section."

I said, "That's true, but two of them were books and not journal articles."

He responded, "I don't care if they were funny books. If you don't have an extensive number of references, you deserve a D."

"Did you read the paper?"

"I don't have time for this. I will not argue with you. Please leave me alone."

Thus endeth the second lesson.

For my next term paper in parasitology, I received an "A". I don't even remember what the subject was. It was a terrible job of slapping together the main point of ideas I got from reading the biological abstracts. I never even read one of the articles, but just their summary. Unfortunately, in order to survive, I had to resort to such subterfuge. One has to adapt to the environment in which one finds himself or herself.

MORE RUDE AWAKENINGS AT UCLA

The hundreds of students in my basic chemistry course were broken up into manageable groups for the laboratories. The laboratories were run by a "TA". "TA" was for Teaching Assistant, who was a graduate student working for a higher degree.

In one of my labs, the TA was saying, "And as you can see", writing on the black board, "this turns into an alpha particle and a mu meson." He paused and then continued, "Oh no. I'm sorry. It turns into a k meson and an alpha particle. Yeah, that's it."

Suddenly, the slightly older student sitting right next to me raised his hand. The TA acknowledged him and the student said very calmly, "No, it turns into a positron and a mu meson."

I thought to myself, "What a cheeky know-it-all. Boy, he is way out in left field, trying to correct the instructor."

The TA immediately rebuked him saying, "No, I'm sure it is a K meson and an alpha particle."

"Well", said the student, "I worked with this problem for two years at Los Alamos in New Mexico and we were the ones who clarified this."

The TA acquiesced. I thought to myself, how could I compete with people with such knowledgeable backgrounds. The competition was indeed tough.

1959

ADDITIONAL RUDE AWAKENING AT UCLA

During my supposed last semester at UCLA I applied for graduation as I had more than enough credits to graduate (I thought). A note in my box a few days later informed me that I did not qualify to graduate because I did not have enough "upper division" units to graduate. I could not take the required number needed during the summer, so I had to come back the next fall to qualify for graduation the next winter.

MOUNT SINAI HOSPITAL EMPLOYMENT

A friend told me that his aunt worked in the admitting office of the Mount Sinai hospital and they needed a part time worker for the daily 6 to 10 pm shift. I applied. During the interview I was asked how fast I could type. I answered, "As fast as these two fingers can go."

She let out a hearty laugh and said, "You're hired. Go over to the personnel office and fill out the forms. Come back and we will go over some things. You start tomorrow night."

Overjoyed at my good fortune, I trotted (skipping along the way) over to the personnel office. As I was filling out the forms, I saw that one of them said I should join the hospital workers union.

I have always hated unions because of the pickets that tried to unionize the steel mill where I worked in Oklahoma City and their dirty tricks. Union organizers threw rocks and bricks at us when we drove into the parking lot. But actually, not to my car because I had a weak battery and was too broke (or cheap) to have it charged up. So I parked about five blocks from the plant on a hill so I could take the brake off and start the car by letting it roll downhill in first gear for a while and then popped the clutch.

Another reason I did not want to join the union was that I would have to pay $50 to join and then I had to pay $15 per month as a member. I only made $1.15 per hour and since I only worked part time, it was like I was just working for the union.

I said, "I don't want to join the union."

The personnel lady looked up at me and said nonchalantly, "Oh, that's all right. You don't have to join the union."

Somewhat surprised by her response, I quickly interjected, "Really; I don't have to join the union?"

She responded, "That's right. You don't have to join the union. You just can't have the job."

Reluctantly, I joined the union.

LIVING IN THE MAID'S QUARTERS

Mount Sinai hospital was almost in Beverly Hills. I saw an ad in the Daily Bruin (UCLA's student newspaper) for a live-in gardener in a Beverly Hills home for $10 per week. So I drove over to this beautiful house on the side of a hill with a gorgeous view of Los Angeles.

The maid's room was off of the garage and had a door that entered into the kitchen of the house. The lady of the house showed me my gardening duties and took me into the kitchen. She opened the cabinet with the dishes and glasses, turn toward me and said, "Are you kosher?"

I thought she was asking if I was from some middle-eastern country like Armenia or Azerbaijan. So I answered, "No ma'am. I'm from Oklahoma."

Looking at me with a quizzical expression she said, "Oh, then you're not Jewish."

I said, "No."

She said, "Then you don't even know what kosher means; do you?" Then she explained to me that it had to do with the dietary restrictions of Jews and that they had to use certain plates and other certain required eating utensils. Boy, did I feel stupid.

THOUGHTS ON MY FIRST AUTOPSY

I had a standing request with the pathologist at Mount Sinai hospital to watch him perform an autopsy. I remember taking a new patient up to the nurse's desk on one of the floors. She was very attractive and very courteous. On her admission slip in the space for diagnosis, it just stated, "observation". When I asked her why she was in the hospital, she said that she was just tired and didn't know the reason and that they were going to do some tests to find out why she was so tired.

A few days later, the pathologist came up to me in the cafeteria and told me to come to his laboratory at 2 pm. When I got there, he said that the patient was a 35 year old female, who had metastasis of a tumor and that he expected to find evidence of the tumor which had spread to the liver, lungs, kidney, pancreas, brain and spinal column. When he pulled away the sheet covering the body, I immediately recognized the attractive lady I had taken up to the nursing station a few days before. She was bald and had obviously been wearing a wig when I saw her earlier.

Just as the pathologist had said, the tumor had spread throughout her body. The liver looked as if someone had shot it with a shotgun as the tumorous tissues were so wide spread. What I found so amazing was the fact that only a few days earlier this lady had seemed outwardly to be so normal. There were no sign that she was so seriously ill.

After observing the entire procedure, I walked back upstairs to the cafeteria. Along the way, everyone that I saw, I thought to myself, "You're dead. You're dead. You are all dead. It is just a matter of time and then we are all dead." This did not particularly depress me. It just seemed like an observable fact that I should recognize. Then I thought that every day is a gift.

ON TO AUSTRALIA AND MY FIRST MARRIAGE

During my time in college, I'd heard several people ask the question, "Which is more educational, four years in college or four years traveling around the world?" Since I now had the one, I wanted the other. Toward the end of my college studies, I sold my 1954 Mercury and bought a $620 steam ship ticket that took me from Los Angeles to London via Australia. Thus, the ticket also paid for my board and room for over two months. I hit a snag in Australia. The snag was called Gail, a beautiful shapely blonde from Sydney. I met her on a ship going from Sydney to London. Gail got off in Adelaide and I jumped ship in Perth (the last stop in Western Australia) and hitch-hiked back to Sydney to be with her.

When we decided to get married, we both found out that her mother hated Americans and said that she wouldn't come to the wedding. The night before, Gail and I got drunk at a party. Gail was begging her mother on the phone to come to the wedding the next day. Her mother adamantly refused. I was so angry that in drunken rage I hit the door leading into a rest room on the hinged side instead of the free swinging side and broke my 5th metacarpal bone in my right hand.

Driving back to a friend of her parent's house, we had an argument and Gail jumped out of the car and I followed her to the house, but she refused to get back into the car. Feeling that I must have broken my hand I drove to a big hospital at 2:30 am. I walked the deserted corridors until I found some folks drinking coffee. They said to follow them, which I did for a while, but I was feeling like I would vomit. I smelled the fresh air from an opened door and just left them to walk on thinking that I was still following them.

When I got outside, I remember seeing this blue hood of a vehicle and put my head onto the hood to rest. After a short period, the hospital personnel came outside, saw me and said loudly, "There he is. Grab him". As I slowly raised up my head, I then noticed that the blue hood belonged to a police car. Well, two burly cops jumped out of the car. One of them grabbed me from behind and twisted my arm behind my back rather forcefully.

I didn't like that, so I took the heal of my shoe and jammed it into the cops tibia (shank), and twirled out of his reach, facing him as he howled. The hospital personnel explained that I had done nothing wrong. They x-rayed my hand and set the bone and put me in a cast.

I went back to my apartment and prepared to get married, but there were several questions in my mind. Would Gail's mother appear? More important, would Gail appear? Well, Gail did appear with her father and the wedding went off without a problem.

The aftermath of the marriage was an interesting situation. My job with a pharmaceutical company involved calling on doctors and dentists all day long. When the doctor would see the cast on my hand, they invariable asked what happened. To begin with I told the truth. I told them that I hit a door. They would usually counter, "Oh, go ahead, mate, you can tell me the truth. What really happened to your hand?" This scenario repeat itself daily.

Just for fun, later on when one of the doctors asked me what happened to my hand, I would respond, "Well, you know the preacher always asks the congregation, does anyone know why these two should not be wed? My future father-in-law, who said he was not coming to the wedding, comes running down the aisle saying loudly, "They've been sleeping together and that is such a sinful thing."

I continued speaking to the doctor, then saying, "I was so mad that I punched him right in the jaw and broke my hand"

Then, the doctors with surprise would usually say, almost with glee to hear such a juicy story, "Really? How interesting." It was just like Hitler said, if you are going to tell a lie, make it a big lie and people are more likely to believe you.

1961

BACK TO THE USA

After one year in Australia I decided to go back to the United States. Gail and I took the P & O steam ship line's Oriana's maiden voyage. When we got back to the USA, I worked for my board and room at the small hotel that my mother owned in Laguna Beach, California, as the night desk clerk.

Seeking a more permanent job, I asked everyone I saw if they knew where I might find a job. Once at an Orange Julius drink stand on Pacific Coast Highway, I asked and was told that I could have a job selling medical equipment at the clerk's brother's company in Santa Ana nearby. Therefore it pays to communicate even with the seemingly unlikely resources at hand. One never knows where opportunities may arise.

A CHANCE CAREER CHANGE

I finally got a good job with a pharmaceutical company (Borroughs-Welcome & Co) as a "detail man", i.e. pharmaceutical service representative. My job was calling on doctors (MDs), dentists, drug stores, pharmacies and hospitals. I would promote our new and existing drugs and give them the details on the new indications for usage and provide feedback to the company on comments by the doctors.

I originally had a desire to go to medical school and was reasonably sure that I could get accepted somewhere. However, when I worked day in and day out, it gradually dawned upon me that I really did not want to be associated with many of the doctors that I called on. They didn't seem to be that interested in their patients and had a most intense interest in how much money they made.

Out of idle curiosity, one day I called on veterinarians, as many of our products although not cleared by the FDA (Food and Drug Administration) for use in animals; I knew that many of the products would be beneficial for animals. The company told us not to bother with veterinarians. But one week, I called on several veterinarians and found them to be like a breath of fresh air. They were actually interested in what I had to say and were much more courteous to me and eagerly wanted to learn about the different products.

Armed with this pleasant experience, I applied to the Veterinary School at the University of California at Davis and was accepted.

71

MY FIRST SON, PHIL ARRIVES AND ALSO POSTPARTUM PSYCHOSIS:

Gail's mother came over for the birth of our son, Philip Sherlock Odend'hal. He was born at Hollywood Presbyterian Hospital on April 25th, 1962. Gail's mother (who had never been to the United States before) and I were asked to leave as they wheeled Gail into the delivery room. We went across the street to a Denny's restaurant and ordered tea, which was given to us separately on a plate with a cup, a small silver container of hot water and a tea bag with a string attached. I happened to glance over to Gail's mother and saw her rip open the tea bag and dump the tea leaves into the hot water.

Gail's pregnancy was not easy and she had been continually agitated about one thing or another. I had requested that the obstetrician give her something to calm her down. He would not do it, as he said it might harm the fetus. After Phil's birth, her anxiety became worse and the fights with her mother became more intense.

One evening I returned home from a short walking visit to a nearby grocery store to find that Gail had left in the car. Her mother who had been drinking heavily was holding the baby and said she had no idea where Gail had gone. Because of my mother-in-law's condition and mouth, I called my friend, Jay Bernstein to come get me and the baby and take me away from this disgusting environment.

Jay took me and the baby to his office in Beverly Hills. I called back to the house periodically to see if Gail had returned. Finally around 11:00 pm she came back. I told her where I was and to come and pick us up. Around 12:00 midnight she drove into the parking lot. I took the baby down stair. To my utter astonishment the car was completely packed with boxes and furniture. Her mother was in the front seat. I gave her the baby and Gail drove off immediately without saying anything.

Dumb founded, I stood in the parking lot and watched them drive away. I did not hear from Gail for three days. I had no idea where she had gone. Finally, she called and said that we had to talk. I asked her where she was. She said that she was staying with an acquaintance in La Canada which is near Pasadena. I thought that was strange, as they really hardly even knew each other and had met each other briefly only once.

Anyway, I drove over to the house and talked with Gail for a short time and she said, "Let's go for a walk." I agreed and we walked over to another quiet residential intersection. She didn't want to leave this intersection for some reason and said rather nonsense statements like, "What about the grass?", "Do you know where you are going?" These statements had no line of reasoning, or made much sense to me at the time.

Suddenly, when a car pulled up to the stop sign, she opened the back door of the car and jumped inside saying, "Hurry, hurry, take me away. He's dangerous." The elderly couple in the car looked at each other, then back at her and drove off.

It was like a nightmare, but I thought the best thing to do was to call the police. I told them that I thought that my wife had a nervous breakdown. They said they thought so too and that she was there at the police station. They advised me to come right down there immediately and that a doctor was there talking with her.

The police informed me that they had received an anonymous phone call earlier complaining that there was a strange man making faces at her and threatening her with ludicrous gestures. She asked them to come to the same intersection (where she had jumped into the car) and arrest the man. They recognized her voice when she came into the police station with her Australian accent.

The doctor told me that if I promised to take her immediately to the psychiatric unit at the Los Angeles County Hospital he would sedate her. Otherwise, he would not release her into my custody. I agreed. After she was sedated she was placed in the back seat of my car, lying down without any restraints what so ever. It was about a 30 to 45 minute drive to the hospital from the police station in La Canada. About three fourths of the way to the hospital driving as fast as I could on the crowded freeways I saw her arms beginning to flay about in the rear view mirror.

Because of her unstable condition, I was petrified that she would wakeup completely and present unmanageable problems while I was driving on the freeways. Luckily, as we drove up to the emergency room entrance, she was only sitting up in a groggy state. They took her away and said that they could hold her for only 72 hours and then they would have to release her to a psychiatrist.

I knew several psychiatrists from my work and one of them agreed to take her case. Gail was transferred to a psychiatric clinic in Hollywood after three days and she remain there for about 10 days of treatment.

When I would visit her in the clinic, I was amazed at the large number of absolutely beautiful young women in the same clinic. The first day I walked into the waiting room I heard one of the women scream, "Help police. They are killing me in here." It was not a happy place.

In a way, a psychiatric illness is worse than a tumor, or serious infection. These conditions can be treated with confidence. There is a history of proven effective methods to accomplish a cure. Unfortunately, there is no sure way to treat many psychiatric disturbances. Thus, it presents a more unsure future and that uncertainty creates a great deal of anxiety.

The psychiatrist recommended that Gail, her mother and the baby go back to Australia as soon as possible. Apparently, Gail had been told repeatedly by her mother that her father was in bad health (not true) and that they all needed to return as soon as possible. I told the psychiatrist, that whatever was his best judgment, I would abide by. So within about a week, they all left for Australia. Phil was two and one half months old at that time.

Two years later, Gail insisted that I get a divorce because I could get it much quicker than she could in Australia. She had refused to return to the US and I had refused to go back to Australia. As she requested, I contacted a lawyer in Sacramento and he started the proceedings.

A few weeks after initiating the process the lawyer called me and informed me that Gail had secured a lawyer in San Francisco to represent her and that I was responsible for her lawyer's fees. I was furious as the divorce was her idea in the first place. My lawyer advised me that I would be responsible for all of the court costs, filing fees and incidentals associated with a trial that might materialize as well.

I said, "I have no idea why she would do such a thing. What does she want?"

The lawyer explained that the San Francisco lawyer said something about she wanted a sewing machine and substantial child support and other items.

I responded, "Tell the lawyer in San Francisco that under the circumstances, I have no intention of paying him a dime."

My lawyer said, "You have no choice. That's the law. You have to pay for your wife's lawyer and court costs."

I said, "You tell that lawyer that I will absolutely refuse to pay him anything. Besides, I have no money and I am a veterinary student with three more years of school. Tell him that I'll go to jail before I give him a nickel."

My lawyer said, "If that is your wish. I will tell him."

The next week he called me and said that the lawyer in San Francisco had dropped the case. The divorce was granted on the grounds of desertion and I was to pay Gail $25 per month child support. Within a few years I increased that sum voluntarily to $50 and then to $80 per month.

1963

VETERINARY SCHOOL; THE FIRST YEAR
Veterinary school was tough, but a lot of fun. Here is one example. Toward the end of the first semester, I was invited to go on a trip to Stanford Research Institute to an island off of the mainland coast of California. Because I missed one of our dissection laboratories, I tried to make it up during the regularly scheduled labs during the next week.

Usually we all worked as teams on formalin injected preserved animal specimens. However, I was issued an intact recently euthanized dog for my makeup lab. The lab that I missed was the male genital tract. Usually the prepared specimens are very hard and not limber at all. My freshly euthanized dog was very pliable and easy to manipulate.

When I opened the abdominal cavity I noticed that the urinary bladder was enlarged, so I squeezed the bladder removing all of the urine. Then I got a syringe and needle and flushed out the bladder several times with plain water. I dissected everything away from the penis, so that it was easily moveable. The dog penis has a rigid bone called the os penis, so it remains sturdy. Thus, I could fill up the urinary bladder with fresh water and easily aim the penis at various objects and squirt the water.

I decided to have some fun. I would call over some of my teammates from their work on the prepared specimens and told them to come over and see something very interesting. They would walk over to my table at the side of the large laboratory. I would point to the enlarged urinary bladder and say, "Look at how large the bladder was when I opened him up."

As they leaned over to get a closer look, I would aim the penis at them and squeeze the bladder shooting the water all over their coveralls. In order to avoid possible fisticuffs or other unfortunate out bursts, I would quickly tell them that it was only fresh water and that I had flushed the bladder out several times. No untoward action resulted from this impractical joke. However, it did have an eventually unexpected adverse consequence weeks later.

We were studying the anatomy of laboratory animals. One of my victims of the urinary bladder assault was a female classmate. She said, "Hey Stew, come over here and look at this live female hamster."

She was holding the hamster on her back in her hand. I walked over and stood in front of her looking down at the hamster. All of a sudden she tickled the hamster's vulva and the hamster peed all over my coveralls. Revenge is sweet she said.

1964

TRANSPORATION PROBLEMS:

I took a job with Dr. William Steinmetz at the Land Park Veterinary Hospital in Sacramento on weekends. I cleaned cages, did general janitorial activities and assisted in surgery on Sundays. So I needed reliable transportation. A classmate owned a 1950 Chevrolet three quarter ton pickup that looked ghastly, but seemed to run okay.

The main thing wrong besides the missing grill in the front, was the listing plywood camper covering the truck bed in the back. It had the appearance of Okies just arriving in California to pick peas. But it worked for my intended purpose of commuting back and forth to Sacramento on weekends.

Burroughs-Welcome & Co rehired me to work for the summer between my freshman and sophomore years. The district sales manager drove over to meet me in Davis to talk about my assignment. I met him at a restaurant just off of the freeway. We met at 10:00 am. Unfortunately, my truck was the only vehicle in the parking lot when he arrived.

After a brief introduction, he asked. "Where is your car? All I see in the parking lot is that old junk wagon out there. Did you walk here?"

I answered, "Oh, that's my truck out there," pointing to the jalopy.

He said, "Oh my goodness, you can't call on doctors and hospitals in that thing. I guess we'll have to rent you a vehicle for the summer."

So when I started to work a week later, I took the bus over to Sacramento. The district sales manager met me and drove to a used car lot and I picked up a Volkswagen beetle. It was hardly much better than the truck. The front end did not latch properly and a common hemp rope secured the front of the hood to the bumper. As I was getting acquainted with the VW, I asked, "Where is the gas gage?"

The used car salesman responded, "You see that little lever down there next to the accelerator?"

"Yep."

77

"Well, when the car starts to cough and lurch, you just turn it over to one side and that allows the reserve gas tank to let you drive another 10 or 15 miles to fill up at the next gas station."

With this piece of priceless essential information, I started out. Believe it or not, I only got about 14 miles from Sacramento when the VW began to cough and sputter. So, I immediately turned the lever next to the accelerator and the car promptly died, as it had run out of gas. The sneaky salesman had already switched the lever and it had drained the reserve tank. Luckily, I ran out of gas exactly even with where I lived in a trailer on this ranch which was only 2 miles from the freeway. One of the ranch hands helped me get the gas to fill up the car.

I hated the VW for several reasons. My job entailed taking a large carrying case with samples and demonstration models into the client's offices. Each time I had to untie and tie the hood down. As I drove along the hood bounced up and down with the wind currents. I drove into San Francisco a couple of times a week to see my girlfriend. As I would drive across the bay bridge the wind was usually so strong that it would blow the VW in one direction and then another and it was hard to keep the light vehicle in the same lane. I was trying to drive straight, but I was constantly changing the steering wheel like I was going around curves in order to stay in the same lane.

One evening when I drove back to my apartment, there was a big crowd gathered around my truck which I had parked in front of the place where I rented a room in a house. There was a police car and a wrecker attempting to attach cables to my truck. I walked up to the policeman who was monitoring the affair and I asked him what was going on. He replied, "Oh, we're just going to tow away this eyesore from this neighborhood."

I responded, "You can't do that because that eyesore belongs to me."

The policeman said, "You can't leave it here. There is a law that states, you cannot leave a commercial vehicle in a residential neighborhood over 8 hours."

"But it is not a commercial vehicle."

"Yes, it is. See the little "E" on the license tag? That signifies that it is a commercial vehicle."

"But I do not use it as a commercial vehicle," I protested.

"It doesn't matter whether or not you use it as a commercial vehicle. It is classified as a commercial vehicle and you can't park it here in this neighborhood overnight."

"Okay then. I will move it."

"Okay, but you have to move it immediately without any hesitation. And if you drive it back here, it will be towed away."

So, I drove around the block to an Alpha Romero dealership and asked the first person I saw, "How much will you give me for my truck as a trade-in?"

He walked outside, opened the hood, checked the tires, started the motor and said, "$300."

I only paid $150 for it and decided that selling it for $300 was a good deal. I looked in the show room and instantly feel in love with an Alpha Romero spider convertible. It was bright red, looked like new and had very low mileage. So, I bought the 1962 Alpha Romero sports car for $1,900.00. My monthly car payment was $87 and the truck was my down payment. I called my district sales manager in Sacramento and told him the story and asked if I could bring back the VW and use the Alpha Romero for work. He agreed. I got work mileage, which more than covered the monthly payments. I was happy all summer.

When I started back to veterinary school in the fall, there was no way I could afford to make the car payments. I traded it (even) on a 1957 Chevrolet station wagon and owed nothing on the Chevrolet.

KIPPER: THE SMARTEST DOG IN THE WORLD
At the Land Park Veterinary Hospital, I would take three dogs, put them in the three outside runs and clean their cages. I'd put them back afterward and do the same thing until all of the cages were cleaned.

There was this one German shepherd that got out every time I would put him in the run. He was the only dog that ever did that.

One day I watched him surreptitiously and saw that he took his nose and would flip up the parallel bar that would hold the gate against the pole next to the door. So, I took a wire and began to wind it around the pole of the door and the pole of the fencing. Lo and behold within a few times, the dog was running loose again. This time I watched and was amazed at his patience (he didn't have much else to do anyway), as he carefully and calmly took his teeth and would eventually unwind the wire and escape the run.

I really liked that dog, so I would just turn him loose when I got to work and let him roam anywhere he wanted to go. He was always courteous to the other dogs and seemed to be just a happy dog. He was there at the veterinary hospital for an unusually long time. I suspected that he was abandoned. Dr. Steinmetz said he could not let me have the dog until he had advertised in the paper for one month that the dog's owner had left him. Then, if there was no response, he could let me have the dog.

After another month, Dr. Steinmetz called and told me that the owner had called him and told him that she did not want the dog any more. She had been in Europe for several months and had just returned. I picked up the dog, named him Kipper, and took him back to my trailer. It certainly was not an ideal place to keep a dog, but was much better than the cage in which he had been incarcerated for months.

As soon as I opened the car door at my trailer park, Kipper jumped out and immediately ran down a cat and caught it under one of the trailers. He shook it like a rag doll and killed it instantly.

The trailer park had recently been purchased and the new owner moved into the house which was on the property. He immediately increased the rent from $19 per month to $25 per month. Everybody was furious. We could understand an increase to $21 or $22, but $25 was considered outrageous.

Shortly after the new owner took over, one evening when I came home some people were trying to set up a new trailer, two pads from mine in

80

the dark. They had this feeble weak flashlight, so I brought them a really good flashlight and told them to bring it back to my trailer when they finished.

Kipper knew (presumably by the foot falls) whether I knew the person approaching my trailer or if he or she was a stranger. Kipper growled, so I knew that a stranger was approaching, and I assumed that it was the new renter. When I opened the door, a man with very thick glasses started to go up the steps into my trailer, but Kipper barked and the man almost stumbled back. I had Kipper on a choke collar and held him firmly.

As the man handed me my flashlight, I asked, "Are you the new renter?"

"No, I am the new owner of the park," he replied.

Immediately on the defensive I quickly said, "Oh, don't worry about my dog. I keep him on a leash, otherwise he would kill every cat in the whole trailer park."

The new owner looked directly into my eyes and said very clearly, "Turn him loose. Turn him loose." We both laughed and became good buddies after that.

There are many other interesting stories about Kipper, but I will just relate one more. On Friday nights a bunch of my classmates and I would go to the Branding Iron restaurant and have a few (sometimes more) beers and enjoy ourselves. So, when I would go home slightly inebriated, since I had had such a good time, I wanted Kipper to have a good time also. Therefore, I would load him into the back of my station wagon and take off into the country side and let Kipper chase rabbits. He had hip dysplasia and never caught the rabbits, but he looked like he was having a good time.

Once in the winter time, I got the car stuck in the mud near the bull barn on the UC-Davis campus. I was freezing and it was a long way back to the trailer park. As I walked along, I saw these Cushman motor scooter golf carts. So, I took out my Lucky Strike cigarette pack, removed the tinfoil and was attempting to hot wire the golf cart so I could get home quicker. Suddenly, there was a spot light in my eyes and I could not see anything. A voice said, "What are you doing?"

I responded, "I'm trying to hot wire this cart, so I can go home. My car is stuck in the mud and I'm freezing."

Well, as it turned out, the flash light was being held by a policemen. He took pity on me and said, "You don't have to do that. I can give you a ride home and save you the trouble of hot wiring the cart."

"Gosh," I replied, "I'll be eternally grateful if you can do that."

Now here is where Kipper's superior intelligence became manifested. I had trained him to never go through any opening (trailer door, car door, fenced-in area, gates, etc.), unless I said "Okay". I had to do this because he had gone through my screen door once.

The kind policeman said, "You can get in the back as I have some junk in the front seat."

As I opened the back door of the police car I asked, "Is it <u>OKAY</u> if my dog rides in the back seat also?" Before I could finish this sentence, Kipper jumped into the back seat with very muddy paws. He hit a bunch of papers lying on the back seat and slid across to the other side of the car hitting the other door with a thud. Mud flew everywhere. The instant he heard "Okay", he thought that it pertained to him and quick as a flash he was through the door.

Luckily it was dark, so the policeman did not see the mud. He said, "It looks to me like the dog has answered that question for me. Since he is already in, let's leave it that way."

1965

RESEARCH ACTIVITY

While I was a freshman at veterinary school, I was fortunate enough to be hired by Dr. Thomas C. Poulter at the Stanford Research Institute to work on the anatomy of seals and sea lions. During the school year I worked on Saturdays describing possible veni-puncture sites and the anatomy of the ear. Toward the end of my freshman year I presented a talk on my work at a conference on diving mammals at Stanford University.

After my talk, a young student about my age approached me and asked me, how did the sea lions regulate the air pressure in their middle ear cavity when they dived. I said that it was an excellent question, but that I didn't know. I could find nothing about it in the scientific literature.

To make a long story short, I worked on several aspect of marine mammal anatomy as a full time summer job between my sophomore and junior years at Davis. On the weekends I continued to work for the Land Park Veterinary Hospital in Sacramento.

One afternoon, I hesitated, but then decided to proceed to break into the middle ear cavity of one of the sea lion specimens that had been injected with blue and red latex used to trace out the arteries (red) and veins (blue).

The ventral bony covering of the middle ear cavity in land mammals, consist of a very thin layer of smooth bone with no foramina (holes which allows passage of arteries, veins, nerves or other tubular structures). In contrast, the ventral bony covering of sea lion middle ear cavities consists of a very thick bone that demonstrated several foramina. When I broke through the bone (not an easy task); I will never forget the exhilarating feeling upon seeing all of the blue latex within the mucous membrane lining the middle ear cavity.

I knew instantly that a collapsible venous sinus in the mucous membrane accounted for the pressure regulation in the middle ear cavity. This discovery eventually resulted in a significant publication in Science magazine in 1966.

The second revelation of my summer employment involved a dead sea lion from the Land Park Zoo in Sacramento. The veterinarian that I worked for was also the attending veterinarian for the zoo. When I showed up (with a terrible hangover), Dr. Steinmetz said, "I have a special present for you today, Stew"

"What's that?"

"Go look in the back room."

What I found was a dead California sea lion wrapped up in a tarpaulin. He told me that the sea lion had died yesterday at the zoo and said that I could have it for my studies. I took it back to school and put it in the pathology refrigerator. Monday morning, I went to the pathology office and requested a necropsy (autopsy in animals). During the necropsy which I observed, I saw large numbers of nematode worms, some still wiggling throughout the fascia (connective tissue) between the skin and underlying muscles.

Quick as a wink, I ran upstairs and told one of the parasitologists to come harvest the worms for identification. She did and after additional efforts on her part, months later she informed me that it was a new previously undescribed species. Further, the traditional convention at that time was to name the species after the discoverer. Thus, the species was named, <u>Dipetolonema</u> <u>odendhali</u> and it was described in a 1967 scientific publication. For these extra curricula activities I was awarded a citation for outstanding undergraduate achievements.

1966

NORTH TO ALASKA

I essentially had three different really good summer job offers from: Stanford Research Institute, Scripts Institute of Oceanography, and the U.S. Fish and Wildlife Service. I chose the latter and went to the Pribilof Islands in the middle of the Bering Sea to assist in a fur seal pup mortality study.

I reluctantly called the person that hired me for the Scripts Institute job and recommended another student who I knew was interested in marine mammals. He said to have the student call him. A week or so later, my friend, Doug Hammond, said that he was hired, thanked me and then said, "Why didn't you warn me that Dr. Elsner stuttered? The long distance charges busted my budget."

The flight from Seattle to Anchorage was interesting. We left Seattle at 8:05 am (local time) and arrived in Anchorage at 8:00 am (local time). So strictly speaking, we arrived in Anchorage 5 minutes before we left

Seattle. The experience in Alaska could fill another book. The wildlife was awesome. We worked 7 days a week, but I still got to observe: artic blue foxes, fur seals, Steller sea lions, caribou, puffins, kittiwakes, murres and Aleuts. I put Aleuts in the same category of wildlife for several reasons. The Aleuts that lived permanently on the island of Saint Paul provided most of the labor involved in harvesting the fur seal pelts.

They all had Russian names, like Alexi Malevidov, and Gabe Russnivishnikov. Every Friday night when we sat down to dinner in the company house (where we lived), we would see a string of Aleuts walking back to their houses in a single file, each with a case of beer on their shoulders. That was the last time that we saw them walking in a straight line until Monday morning.

There were just too many interesting incidents to cover in this section, but one stands out more than any of the others. Our boss had loaned Jerry Wharton (the other veterinary assistant) and I to the tagging team. This group was understaffed. The procedure was as follows: Some of the Aleuts would isolate the 150 to 200 pound bachelor male fur seals into a compact mob. Then Jerry and I would go to work. We alternated the duties. One of us had a long sturdy pole with a thick heavy rope attached very firmly to the end. The pole person would make a noose and slip it over the head of the fur seal and twist it tightly around his neck. Then (this wasn't easy), the fur seal's head would be forced to the ground and restrained there, while the next procedure was performed.

The next procedure involved one of us to jump on the back of the fur seal, put both knees on the pectoral flippers and like riding a bucking bronco attempt to hold the animal down, while one of the Aleuts would dash in and affix a coded tag to the rear of one of the flippers.

As one can imagine, after 10 or 20 of such operations, the procedure became pretty exhausting. On one occasion I jumped onto the back of this fur seal and somehow he turned his head around and clamped down on my knee.

Jerry looked down and said, "Hey Stew, he's got you by the knee."

"You think, I don't know this?" I calmly said.

"But you're not doing anything about it," Jerry stated.

I replied, "I can't. He's got me by the knee,"

The minute that he bit me, I hesitated to try and pull away too drastically. I was frightened that such an action on my part might result in a ripping of my flesh if he resisted. Therefore, I patiently waited for some time and then he voluntarily opened his mouth and I could pull my knee away. I still have a very distinct scar where his canine tooth entered the medial aspect of my knee.

The last Sunday we were there, we didn't have to work and we attended the Russian Orthodox Church. The church was located on the hill in the town of St. Paul and the entrance to the church had a hand written sign that said in English, "Please, no drinking during the services".

The service lasted three hours. Everyone except, Jerry Wharton and I went up to the front and kissed a picture of Jesus Christ. There were no pews, so the devotees had to stand the whole time. We stayed the whole time ourselves. At the conclusion of the services, as the Aleuts walked out, you could see empty beer cans being kicked about and people stumbling over a few crushed beer cans.

When the absolutely amazing summer was over, one of the other student workers from Colorado and I traveled from Anchorage to Fairbanks, stopping at Denali National Park, hoping to see Mount McKinley. While we didn't see the mountain, we did see: grizzly bears, Dal sheep, caribou, eagles, and lots of other birds.

Our plane was to leave Fairbanks at 2:30 am. So to kill some time we went to see the movie Mary Poppins. When we walked out of the theater around midnight, I glanced up into the night sky and was completely dumbfounded. I had never ever experienced such a sight in my life, i.e. the northern lights (aurora borealis). It was as if some supernatural being took a giant huge purple drapery and shook it back and forth interspersed with yellow-green lights flickering in between. It is impossible to adequately describe.

86

MARRIED THE BARMAID:

About six weeks before I graduated from veterinary school I met a cute barmaid. Bobbie was a sociology student and she was to graduate with a bachelor's degree. She was going to join the Peace Corps and go to Nepal. I had just accepted a job with the School of Hygiene and Public Health at Johns Hopkins University and I was going to India.

Since we were headed in the same direction and our hormones were excited about getting together over there, we decided to get married. The week after graduation we went to Reno and were married by the justice of the peace. Two of my classmates went with us as witnesses. Bob Mckittrick was from San Diego and Dester Aturo was from Nigeria. Bob was very white and Dester was very black. When they took a photograph that evening of us all together to document the ceremony, all you could see of Dester was a set of white teeth.

DR. POULTER'S OFFER:

Dr. Thomas C. Poulter was the chief investigator of an Office of Naval Research grant at the Stanford Research Institute. He hired me to do research on sea lions to describe the anatomy of the larynx and middle ear and to search for veni-puncture sites. He was second in command of Admiral Bryd's Antarctic explorations in the 1930's and was one of the most modest and amazing individuals with whom I have had the pleasure of an association.

As I neared graduation from veterinary school, he offered me a job to come and work full time with him on his grant. I was honored and pleased. I told him that I would have to think about it, as I had a very good offer from Johns Hopkins University to go to India with a project on public health.

I will never forget his kind statement. When he finished telling me about his wish that I join his research team he said, "Nothing would please me more." I felt bad, later on, when I told him that I had decided to go to Johns Hopkins. Again, I will never forget his statement. He said, "I don't blame you because that is probably what I would do also."

ON TO JOHNS HOPKINS

Being madly in love, but also sensitive individuals, we drove down to Southern California to introduce our newly acquired spouse to our respective parents, who had no idea what had taken place. That is another story.

We drove to Baltimore. I called Dr. Chuck Southwick, the man who had hired me. "We're here," I said over the phone.

"Well that's good. Wait a minute; you said, 'we're here'. What do you mean 'we're'? Who is with you?" he stammered.

"My wife. We got married right after we both graduated," I responded proudly.

"Oh, no, we didn't budget for a wife. I don't know what we are going to do."

"I'll pay for her ticket to India. So don't worry."

"It isn't just a question of a ticket. There are strict forms to fill out, visas, passports and tons of paper work involved. Oh what the hell, come on in and we'll figure it out."

ON TO AFRICA

The Department of Pathobiology had received a grant to form a research group called, the Center for Medical Research and Training (CMRT). The area of study was India. After a month of orientation in Baltimore, we were off to India. I asked the administrator if we could go by way of Rome (to see experts at the Food and Agriculture Organization [FAO]) and then to Africa (to see wildlife). To my surprise, he agreed.

Early the first morning in Rome, I called a veterinarian at FAO and made an appointment. He told me to go to the train station and take a taxi. At the taxi stand I said to the taxi driver, "F, A, O", pronouncing each letter very distinctly.

The taxi driver said something back that I could not understand at all. But we continued to talk to each other with neither of us understanding the other.

He seemed like a pleasant sort, so I got into the taxi. We drove around Rome and the taxi driver would periodically point out the sights and say such things as, "circus maximus, capitol, casa palatino, vatican". Then suddenly turning a corner, he pointed out a very large white building and said, "Fao".

I thought he said, "Fowl."

Using my ruptured Spanish I said quickly, "Que, que?", hoping he would translate my Spanish into what, what?

Again he said, "Fao".

It then dawned upon me the FAO was called "fao" by the locals.

Bobbie and I stayed in Nairobi for one week. We saw Nairobi National Park, Amboseli National Park and thoroughly enjoyed ourselves. I took lots of pictures. I wanted to go to the Serengeti National Park in Tanzania, but we could not afford the time or the money.

Three incidents from the African trip are particularly memorable. The first one was the time that Bobbie and I were walking along a concrete walkway at the Nairobi Zoo. There was a single step that Bobbie did not see and she fell. I had just turned around to tell her something and she had completely disappeared (on the ground).

The second was that I had read a book by George Schaller called the "Year of the Gorilla" and he was on the staff in the Department of Pathobiology. I wrote to him and asked for him to recommend a moderately priced hotel where we could stay while we were in Nairobi. He wrote back and told us about this one hotel and we stayed there.

We were not in Calcutta more than a week when I got this very apologetic letter from George saying how sorry he was for recommending that particular hotel, as he said he learned later that it was essentially a whore house. I wrote back to him and assured him that we had no problem with the place at all and that it was more than satisfactory in every way. We had seen no evidence that it operated as a whore house.

The third incident of disappointment involved a slide show. The resident coordinator of the Hopkins research program in Calcutta , Nat Pierce and his wife had been trekking in Nepal and had just received their slides back from the photography store. I said that we had just received our slides from the photos that I had taken in Africa. So we had a dinner party to show our respective slides. All of the Hopkins personnel were invited.

Nat showed his slides, which were excellent. Beautiful scenes of the Himalayas and all were carefully composed. I showed mine next and here is an example of my commentary.

"Oh gosh, they looked so big at the time. But if you look in the background, see that little thing that looks like a tree on the horizon? That's a giraffe." And ,"Look in between the bushes there that dull grey color just visible is an Ostrich." And further, "You can't see the lions very well, but they are those tan colored things that look like mole hills next to the lake." It was an embarrassing experience. I vowed to buy a telephoto lens before I went anywhere again.

INDIA
In India I kept a diary and wrote in it every single day, except when I had hepatitis and was under house arrest for two months. Someone told me that whenever you go someplace new and exotic you should write everything down the minute you get there while it is fresh and new to you. If you don't do that, after a while, the newness wears off and you no longer notice the things that impressed you to begin with. India was truly an experience of a lifetime. So many interesting things happened that I would need to write two books at least.

I could not begin to scratch the surface of describing even a small percentage of the wonder that I saw. To begin with, I was petrified by the kamikaze taxi drivers. They seemed at several horrifying moments to have a strong death wish. Miraculously, I survived many near misses.

90

The Communist Party of India (CPI) was in control of the state of West Bengal and Jhoti Basu was the Chief Minister the day we arrived. The next day Indira Ghandi (the Prime Minister of India at that time) declared "Presidency rule" and kicked out Jhoti Basu and the CPI and riots broke out. On our second day at the New Kennilworth hotel, I was awakened from my jet lag during a lunch time snooze by gun shots and the roar of what sounded like a cannon.

I will never forget opening out the shutters of the hotel window and seeing the street pavement hardly visible there were so many people running down the street. Then a large truck pulled into the intersection a half a block away and about 30 to 40 soldiers piled out and began firing their rifles above the heads of the running people. I quickly shut the shutters. We went up to the roof to watch the riot. However, as soon as we got to the top, the tear gas blew our way and we made a hasty retreat back to our respective rooms. Many people died and the riots continued for several days.

1968

 Too many highlights to mention, but the over whelming most interesting two events were the Peace Corps conference at the Southeastern Railway Hotel in the coastal city of Puri in the state of Orissa and the three weeks trekking in Nepal.

PURI PEACE CORPS CONFERENCE
Shortly after meeting the Peace Corps couple (Joe and Deedee Sly) that lived in our study village of Singur in Hooghly District (about an hour's train ride northwest of Calcutta), they invited my wife and I to attend their "Year End Conference" in Puri. This invitation was issued during a most unusual train ride into Calcutta about two months before the conference.

The American Consulate in Calcutta was having a special affair to honor the Peace Corp volunteers in the state of West Bengal. Joe and Deedee and Bobbie and I were all dressed up and decided to take the train into Calcutta instead of taking the Jeep. We were standing on the platform in Singur (along with the other thousand or so Bengalis).

When the train arrived, everyone was making mad dashes to enter the opened doorways. As we tried to enter the car in front of us, several Bengalis inside the car said something in frantic Bengali.

I said to Joe (who had been in India for a year and was supposed to know Bengali), "What are they saying?"

Joe replied, "I don't know".

While the Bengalis were adamant and even tried to push us away from the door, the horn for immediate departure sounded and we all got into that car. Suddenly, once inside, it became apparent why they tried to prevent us from entering. There was at least an inch of water covering the entire floor of that railway car.

The source of the water was derived from the "Channa" that was carried in baskets lined with what looked like checkered dishtowels. Water was constantly added to the basket to keep the "Channa" moist, but it also leaked out constantly. "Channa" is the curdled milk rich in protein. It is used to prepare the sweetmeats by confectioners in Calcutta.

Recognizing the substantial layer of water covering the entire floor of the car, we all tiptoed to the rear of the car and took some of the empty seats; no other passengers were present. As soon as we sat down, the train took off from the station quite rapidly. Because we had not had time to think about the consequences, the inertia of the water wanted to stay situated at the location of the station and a wall of dirty water came flowing rapidly toward the back of the car where we were sitting. It sloshed against the back wall and bounced off, splashing all of us with dirty water.

Like a conditioned reflex, we all got up at the same time groaning and moaning and headed for the front of the compartment, as more water slopped against the back wall. As we discussed our ill-fated luck of entering this particular car, the train began to slow for the next station and abruptly hit the brakes. Once again, because of inertia, the water then took a forward motion and once again before we could stand up, drenched us with the water slopping against the front wall of the compartment.

It was very embarrassing, as all of us were college graduates who had studied physics, and knew in theory about inertia. From that day, I have always paid more attention to someone who is trying to tell me something, even though I might not understand immediately.

At the Year End Peace Corps conference in Puri, I reported on my project which at the time was devoted to conducting a census of the humans and domestic animals in a specific geographical area. When the director of the program told me to do this, I had responded, that I did not spend four years in veterinary school to count cows. I was mollified by his response that one cannot report on disease prevalence or incidence, unless the basic population of cattle had been determined and that was the major need of the day. At the conference I also requested that the volunteers that might be assigned to villages near me, to let me know of any veterinary problems they might find.

The other presenter on the program was the Peace Corp doctor. He reported on his passion, which was Indian art and gave a lengthy presentation with great details that might have interested 0.01% of those present.

The Southeastern Railway Hotel was right on the beach and had a delightful environment. On the one free afternoon, some went swimming and others wanted to go to the big market and do some shopping. Shopping bores me silly, so I decided to go to a wildlife park many miles away by bus by myself.

At the bus station, I bought my ticket and got on the bus. The bus was not scheduled to leave for about 30 minutes and there were only three others on the bus initially. I took a seat in the back of the bus and just looked around. There were tea stalls, food hawkers and many folks transporting produce in the surrounding area.

What caught my eye was the large elephant that was begging. The mahout guiding the begging business on top of the elephant's head, turned the elephant eventually to the bus. On my side of the bus, there was one man reading the newspaper. Country buses in India have no glass in the windows.

The elephant slowly and quietly approached the window of the man reading the newspaper, raised his trunk, aimed the tip of his trunk directly into the man's ear and blew forcefully into it. The unsuspecting man threw his paper into the air and screamed loudly and then obviously cursed the elephant and the mahout.

Back at the hotel, I noticed a group of Russian visitors. When I casually tried to engage one of the stragglers of the group into a conversation, he essentially ignored me and did not respond. Later on I was told by an American consulate person that the Russian was not being rude. He was just protecting his rear, by not saying anything. It seems that if he was seen talking with me, he would have to write a full report of everything that was said. If he didn't write the report, he would be under suspicion for some crime against the state or something.

There is a huge Hindu temple in Puri called the Jagannath temple. It is devoted to the worship of Vishnu and Krishna. It was said that there were 5,000 Hindu priests that actually lived at the temple. It was apparently particularly visited by folks that were having trouble conceiving a child. The bigger the gift that they gave to the temple; the better their chances were of having a baby later on; it was said.

An interesting aspect of the trip down to Puri by train, illustrates some unique marketing strategies. We took the overnight train trip leaving Calcutta Wednesday evening January 19th. When we arrived in the Puri train station, I noticed the exact same newspaper that I had read the day before in Calcutta, in a stack next to the door. The only difference was that the date on the newspapers sent to Puri was dated Thursday, January 20th.

Another interesting aside was a trip to the pharmacy. There were packets of condoms for sale. On the outside of the small boxes, written in English as well as the local language was, "Use only once".

MR. E. P. GEE AND
THE CERTIFICATE OF EXISTENCE

Mr. E. P. Gee wrote a book on *The Wildlife of India*. He was also on the board of directors of the World Wildlife Fund. I met him at the Calcutta Zoo after a wildlife meeting. When he found out that I was a veterinarian, he asked me to come to his home in Shillong, in the eastern Indian state of Assam to write a grant proposal to study the possibility that brucellosis was limiting the swamp deer population.

I agreed and Bobbie and I flew to Assam and spent three days at his house. Sitting down for lunch one day, Mr. Gee got this far off stare in his eyes and he said, "The Bank of England is driving me out of my mind. They will not send me my pension."

"Why not", I enquired?

"They say that they never got my certificate of existence for June," he responded.

"What's a certificate of existence? I've never heard of that before."

"Well, you see I am a retired tea planter. I've been here in Shillong almost all of my life. My pension comes monthly from the Bank of England and every month I have to send in the mail a statement saying that, I am alive and well in Shillong and then they send me the money."

At this point, the veins over his temple area began to bulge and his face turned a slightly red color. He continued his saga, "And the bloody idiots have no brains at all. I wrote to them and asked them if they received my certificate of existence for July. They wrote back and said, yes they did receive my certificate of existence for July, but before they could pay for July, they had to have a certificate of existence for June."

His veins began to bulge even more and his face became redder, "I wrote back and said to the idiots, 'If I was alive in July, surely my good man you must realize that I had to be alive in June, so send me my money."

"I got this pitiful letter yesterday, saying that they acknowledged that I must be alive in July, but they could not send any money until they received my certificate of existence for June."

This visit to Shillong occurred in August. I returned to Calcutta and had the secretary type up the grant and sent it to Mr. Gee. He would forward it with his approval to the World Wildlife Fund headquarters

95

and let me know the results as soon as he could. Unfortunately, I never heard from him again. After several weeks, I wrote to him and received no reply. I could not understand his silence.

In November, Bobbie and I were trekking in Nepal. On the way back to Kathmandu, I met an environmentalist and I asked him if he knew Mr. E. P. Gee. He indicated that he knew him. I said, "He's a funny duck."

I was just about to go into my story, when the fellow interjected, "Actually, he is a dead duck. He died recently."

So, ironically, he must have died shortly after we left his house in August or September. The question of his missing certificate of existence probably was never resolved in his life time. Who knows, perhaps the battle over the certificate of existence may have been what killed him.

TREKKING IN NEPAL

November is the best time to go trekking, as the monsoon season is over and the days are much more cool and fresh with less chance of rain. We flew to Kathmandu, the capital of Nepal and spent a couple of days sightseeing. There was a huge white building where the king lived. It was said to have over 300 rooms to house his concubine. This was so he could enjoy a new woman every night if he wanted, taking time off probably for some of the official holidays.

Bobbie and I went to visit the Swayambhunath Temple just outside of Kathmandu. We had sling bags with our lunch which consisted of sandwiches and some bananas. At this huge Buddhist temple there were lots and lots of Rhesus monkeys running around all over the place. When we took out our food, the monkeys attacked us and dove into the sling bags stealing our bananas. I literally had to beat them off. We retreated out of the temple grounds and walked about a half mile down the road back towards Kathmandu to a tea stall to finish our lunch and to have some tea.

At the tea stall, there was one area with chairs arranged around a "U" shaped table. All of the chairs were taken, except for two places which Bobbie and I were quick to occupy. Almost everyone else sitting appeared to be hippies. They were passing around a small device that looked like the top of the real old locomotive smoke stack with what looked like coals in the top. Each person took a deep drag from the bottom, held the smoke in their lungs for a moment or so and slowly exhaled. When the person passed it on to me, I said, "No, thanks.", and started to pass it on.

The young man looked at me with big doe like eyes and said in English, "Don't you smoke?"

I replied, "Yeah, I smoked for 15 years and just gave it up last year."

His eyes got even bigger and he said, "Like man that's cool. Like you smoked pot for 15 years and gave it up?"

"No", I responded, "I smoked Lucky Strikes for 15 years and gave it up."

There were hippies all over the place in Kathmandu. Some of them were even begging and were a pest to the local inhabitants. The government was trying to kick many of them out of the country.

After a couple of days, we flew to Pokhara about 300 miles west of Kathmandu. Just before we landed, there were local Nepalis who were in charge of running the cows off of the grass runway (where they had been grazing) so the plane could land safely. When we stepped out of the plane, it was surrealistic to see the mountain tops which were covered with snow mixed in and above the big white puffy clouds.

We stayed at the Paramount Hotel near the airport. It was owned by a Peruvian ex-monk. He told fascinating stories. For instance, he said that he joined a Buddhist monastery for 6 months and spent his time checking the speed of the bed bugs as they crawled across the cobble stone floor of his cell.

He said, after one month of solitary confinement, one day when he came down for breakfast, the abbot said, "It is time."; meaning that he could say a few words about the significant meditations and contemplations he had undergone during the first month of reflecting upon the meaning of life, etc.

He responded, "Bed hard."

At the end of the next month, again the Abbot said, "It is time."

He said, "Food bad."

At the end of the next month, the Abbot said, "It is time."

He said in a loud voice so all could hear, "I quit".

The Abbot then said equally forcefully, "Thank God. All you have done since you have been here, is bitch, bitch, bitch."

The owner arranged for us to have Trapoon, as our Tibetan porter. He carried our supplies, including a large jug of drinking water and a back pack with our change of clothes. We paid him 7 rupees per day (about $2 a day at that time) and paid for his food along the way. He was also our guide and took us on the Jomsom trail toward the province of Mustang, up the Kali-Gandoc River valley.

Pokhara is at 2,600 feet above sea level and the peak of Machapuchari mountain (only about 20 miles away) is 26,000 feet above sea level. Trapoon said that when the Tibetans escaped from the Chinese in 1959 and went to the Tibetan refugee camp near Pokhara, there were no births for two years and half of the refugees died the first year.

We trekked over two mountain passes, over several damaged suspension bridges and up the Kali-Gandoc River for about 10 days. We stayed in the homes of local villagers. These people were referred to as Tagalis. They allowed trekkers to stay in their homes for no charge, but the food consumed had to be paid for. The amount charged was higher than what the Tagalis paid for it to make their hospitality profitable.

At one house, when we came down for breakfast, there were large rounded globs of what looked strangely similar to brown dog turds on the eggs. Hesitating to eat, until I had clarified my suspicion, I asked Trapoon what the brown stuff was. After conferring with the home owner, he told the following story. Their son had joined the Gurkha soldiers and fought for the British during the second world war. Every time he came home, he always brought a couple of jars of peanut butter, which they all relished as a delicacy. The peanut butter on the eggs was not bad, although I have never tried it since then.

The scenery was magnificent and some of the pathways were dangerous with very steep drop offs. Interestingly, on the trek back over the same route, many of the pathways had been washed away, or just eroded and the new path was very narrow and scary.

I came across a veterinary clinic half way up the Kali-Gandoc River valley. I enquired about the diseases of cattle and buffalo in the area. The animal health worker said that they had seen the first cases of Foot and Mouth Disease (FMD) in the last year or two and they had never had FMD in the valley before.

I asked him, how did they suspect that the FMD got there. He said that in the past, the villagers in the area never went down into the Terai region (the relatively flat land at the base of the Himalayas), because of the evil spirits that inhabited there. [The evil spirits were mainly malaria that was endemic because of the mosquitoes]. He added, that since the evil spirits had disappeared from the Terai, then the villagers went down to the Terai with their cattle and buffaloes and that is where the FMD came from.

The evil spirits (malaria) had been eradicated by spraying with DDT which killed the mosquitoes (the vectors of the disease). It is ironic that a successful human public health program eventually lead to a detrimental veterinary public health problem.

Another outstanding observation was the Tagali women's dress. They looked almost identical to the Navajo native American dress. They had long pleated skirts and wore velvet blouses. We passed and were often passed by women carrying huge loads of material in their baskets suspended on their backs by thick head straps. We met very few non-Nepali trekkers on our journey of three weeks.

PRESUMED HOMOSEXUAL WAS NOT

Once a week, I would go into Calcutta for an administrative meeting with the other Johns Hopkins researchers. I began taking the train because it was faster and easier than driving through all of the congestion and traffic jams. The only place in India where I saw a regular line was at the taxi stand outside of Howrah train station. There was a line there to maintain order and they had a policeman at the end of the line to assign each waiting person to individual taxis.

The first time I got into that line with 50 to 100 other waiting taxis customers, the man behind me pressed up against me with his body. I thought to myself, 'Oh my goodness, I have a queer person behind me.' As the line advanced slowly toward the end and people would step forward, he would repeatedly press up against my body. After about three or four big shifts like that, I would take my solid brief case and hit him quite hard in the shin of his leg. So he did stop pressing up against me.

The next week, lo and behold, another homosexual was behind me pressing his body up against mine. And once again, I would clobber his shin bone with my brief case. When the same thing occurred the following week, it finally dawned upon me that these dudes were not homosexuals at all. It was a cultural survival technique. If the people outside of this regulated line did not press up against the next person, they couldn't go anywhere. So I just adjusted to the fact that this was the way things were in India and it ceased to bother me anymore. I figured that it was easier for me to just tolerate it, instead of trying to change the cultural habits of 350 million Indians.

1969

1969 was an indescribable fantastic experience, filled with unusual occurrences. I experienced dengue fever, hepatitis, amebic dysentery, rice water stools, unknown fevers and unknown periods of general malaise. But I thoroughly enjoyed the period of wellness in between the rough spots. The veterinary and ecological studies have been previously reported in various publications. Many of the people that I worked with have died and I still keep in touch with those still hanging around. There are just too many stories to tell.

ELECTION TIME IN WEST BENGAL
The two outstanding events that occurred during 1969 in West Bengal were; the general elections and the showing of a film on America

putting a man on the moon. There were three communist parties in West Bengal vying for power: the Communist Party of India (CPI), the Communist Party of India-Marxist (CPI-M), and the Naxalites (who were Maoists revolutionary terrorists). All of these different communist political parties were killing each other daily according to the newspaper accounts.

In Singur, I lived directly across the street from the soccer field. They had a political rally there one night with thousands of people attending. The chief minister from the state of Kerala (another Indian state with an elected communist government) was the featured speaker. He said that just as the British had taken control of India by sending agents to snatch key real estate in outlying villages; that is what America was attempting to do with the Americans living in Singur.

The next day, a very perplexed 14 year old boy who collected postage stamps from me, told me about these accusations. I just laughed and told him that they were not true. Still, he was very upset and said that I should get out of town because there may be some trouble, as many folks were irritated and believed the chief minister.

Therefore, I sent a message to Dwain Parrack (at the biological field station) and Gordon Dean (at the hook worm research station) and told them to come to my house that evening to discuss the situation as the election was to occur in two days and more rallies were scheduled in Singur.

We all assembled in my house that evening after dinner. As we were discussing the various options of whether to: remain in Singur, go to Calcutta, or take a short vacation out of state; a crowd gathered outside the front of my house. In loud voices the mob chanted either; "Who owns this property.", or "Vote for Gopal Banerjee" (he was the communist candidate). We honestly could not figure out what exactly they were saying, but we knew they were not wishing us a happy birthday.

It was a little unnerving. Since I was the one with the largest public exposure, I decided that Bobbie and I would retreat to Calcutta until the elections were over. I was out every day in the surrounding villages and came into contact with Gopal Banerjee (the CPI candidate) and had been threatened a few times by communists. Gordon and Dwain decided to remain inside their research compounds which were much more secure than my house.

The night of the elections, the American Consulate was showing the film of the landing on the moon at a large theater in Calcutta, which was heavily attended by many invited local dignitaries. When I walked into the lobby, Narayan Alim (Johns Hopkins administrator) walked up to me and said, "I just got a phone call from Singur. Dwain and Gordon are surrounded by a mob and they are saying that tonight is the night to fight the foreigners."

"How long ago was this?" I asked.

"Just as I left the office to come here. We were cut off and I tried to call them back, but could not get through," he responded.

At that moment the American consulate general came through the front door and I grabbed him and told Narayan, "Tell the consulate general what you just told me."

The consulate general listened intently and then turned to another American in his party and said, "Handle this situation immediately."

The man looked at me and said, "Follow me."

We went outside and hailed a taxi and drove straight to the American Consulate. During the drive with the streets clogged and various vehicles blocking our progress, the man swore in Hindi to the cab driver to hurry up.

After arriving at the Consulate, the man went to the consulate generals living quarters and got on the phone to call the police in Chinsura, which was the district government headquarters. Unfortunately, he could not get through. We tried to call Singur and also could not get through.

When I asked him what his plans were, he said that he wanted to send tanks from Chinsura to Singur to protect the Americans. I thought at the time that it might have been a little overkill, but he was the expert.

In the end, after about an hour of trying to call anyone anywhere, we gave up and went back to the film, which ended as soon as we took our seats in the theater.

The next day, back in Singur, Dwain and Gordon said, they were just drinking beer and having fun. They acknowledged calling Narayan. Similar to the experience at my house a few days before, it was difficult to understand what the slogans by the chanting Bengalis meant.

LEARNING TO LIE

My field work involved going to every house hold in ten small villages and conducting a census of humans and animals. However, in the three Muslim villages, I was not permitted to go house to house. I had to go to the mosque and wait for the head of each household to come to me and I had to conduct the interviews there.

The mosque consisted of a flat cement area with no walls or demarcation around it. As I was obviously an unusual sight being white skinned there was always a crowd of men and boys surrounding me during the interviewing process. One of the reasons that I could not go house to house, is that the Muslims did not want me to see any of their women or young girls.

By the time of the third survey, I was able to conduct the interviewing in Bengali, so my three Hindu assistants were just standing next to me, as I interviewed each householder. At the conclusion of one interview, I took out the results of the previous interview from 9 months before and asked the following question in my halting grammatically incorrect basic Bengali, "Eight year old female white cow, with one horn bent backward; what happened to her?"

Before, the householder could respond, a small boy about 10 years old said in very clear voice, "*Amra kay-eh-chi*", which means in Bengali, "We ate her."

"No, no, no," everyone said standing around him.

I will never forget the wonder in the small boy's eyes, as he insisted to everyone, "Of course we ate her. You all know that."

103

He was suddenly whisked away out of sight and removed from the gathering. The grown men, continued to insist that the little boy did not know what he was saying and was perpetually telling false stories.

As we left the village, I asked my Hindu assistants, if they thought that the boy was telling the truth. Each said, that they thought that the boy told the truth, but that it was very dangerous to say the truth, especially around Hindus. They acknowledged that Muslims do kill cows in the confines of their own villages and that did not upset them, as long as they didn't think about it.

I said that since the Muslims were in their own village and there were not any other Hindus around besides us, it turned out all right. But I asked what would have happened, if the boy had said it in a crowd of Hindus. They said that the Hindus would have been furious.

So, I concluded that essentially, the young boy, learned to lie right then and there. The truth could be a hazard to one's health in different circumstances.

DON'T STEP ON MY SHADOW

In the village of Paltagar, I was talking with a person about the health of his cow. He was very upset and concerned. We were standing on the north entrance to a bridge and the afternoon sun cast our shadows completely across the bridge entrance. As we talked, I noticed an old lady and little girl patiently standing, apparently waiting to cross the bridge.

After some time, the old lady said to the man in Bengali, "Please Dada (meaning older brother), let us cross the bridge."

The man then walked to the eastern side of the bridge, and as his shadow was no longer cast across the entrance to the bridge, the little old lady and young girl then walked across the bridge.

I asked my assistant what that was all about. He explained that the man was a Voishnob, a higher holy man and that it was bad luck to step on his shadow. I said that he would not even have known if they did step on his shadow. My assistant said that the old lady and girl would have known and they just could not do it for fear of bad luck and/or punishment in this or the next life.

COINCIDENCE IN DARJEELING

Bobbie and I went to Darjeeling, a town in the foothills of the Himalayas in the most northern part of West Bengal. It is a beautiful hill station where the British went to relax in the summer time. There are excellent views of the Himalayan snow covered peaks. We stayed at a delightful hotel called the Windameyer.

We spied a nice restaurant in town and went inside. We had already had lunch, but it looked so inviting that I walked up to the matre d' and asked, "Would it be possible to make a reservation for dinner tonight around 8 pm?"

He looked at me (probably sizing me up for a bribe) and stated, "I am so sorry sir, but we do not make reservations here."

I countered, "I don't understand why not. We don't want to come back here and have to wait a long time for a table."

"We serve people on a first come, first serve basis. If you come a little earlier; say around 7:00 or 7:30 tonight, I can assure you that we will have a tables available for you and you will not have to wait."

So, a little after 7 pm, we arrived at the restaurant and I walked up to the same man and asked if there was a table available. He explained, if we would prefer not to share a table, it would be a substantial wait. However, if we shared a table with someone else, we could be seated immediately. We chose the latter course.

He put us at a table that was occupied by one single young looking white person, and we had not seen many of that variety in town at all. I said, "Where are you from?"

He answered, "The United States."

"That's where we're from," I said and then asked, "Are you in the peace corps?"

"Yes," he replied.

"Here or in Nepal?"

"Nepal."

"Then what are you doing in India?"

"I'm on my way to go to Calcutta tomorrow and then I am going to meet my twin brother in Hong Kong."

"Where 'bouts are you from in the United States?"

To my surprise, he said, "Oklahoma."

"That's where I'm from," I stammered. "Where 'bouts in Oklahoma?"

"Oklahoma City."

Even more surprised I added, "That's where I'm from. What high school do you go to in Oklahoma City?"

"Casady High school."

Astounded, I said with excitement, "That's where I went to high school. What's your name?"

"Ross Anthony."

"Is your father Guy Anthony?"

"Yes, but how on earth did you know that?"

"Because my mother told me that when she was in high school she wanted to marry your father, but someone else beat her to it."

"Oh my goodness, please do not tell your mother that you met me here and that I was going to go to Hong Kong. I don't want anyone to know."

Incredibly, almost a quarter of a century later, my mother would end up falling in love with Guy Anthony's brother, Ray, at her 62nd high school reunion and living the rest of her life with him.

1970

TRIP BACK HOME

We flew to Bombay. We spent a couple of days at Alora and Ajanta caves in Madra Pradesh which is an amazing place. The temples there were carved out of volcanic Amigdaloid trap rock. One of the temples was worked on continuously for 20 generations.

I took a side trip to the Gir Forest in the state of Gujarat. A researcher there was studying the Gir forest lions. He wanted my input on his interesting project. That was an experience for sure in many ways. Then on to Tel Aviv and a few days traveling around to see the Negev desert, Bethlehem, Beersheba and other sights.

DELPHI IN GREECE

From Israel we flew to Athens, Greece. I had purchased a goat skin covered drum from a man in a bar in Jerusalem after enjoying a few drinks. I had it slung over my shoulder as we walked past a security guard at the Athens airport; the security guard just started walking along with me and beat on the drum. Greeks are very expressive and uninhibited people.

One day we took a tour by bus to Delphi. It is where the old oracle used to hang out with Zeus and the other gods. The tour guide was a very attractive young lady who looked and acted like a movie star. She was very good looking, so it was easy to pay attention to her. After touring the main museum, she took us down the hill to a spring that gushed forth from a slit in the rocky side of a sheer cliff on the side of the mountain.

She said, "Oh, how disappointing, the group of old people that are usually here are not here today."

She continued, "It is said that this spring provides miraculous water and acts sort of like the fountain of youth and that is why there are almost always a bunch of old people gathered around. The last time I was here, I asked one of the old people if he drank from the spring regularly. He answered, 'Yes, I drink from the spring every day and I have honey every day at breakfast, lunch and dinner time.' When I asked him how old he was, he responded, 'I'm 79 years old.'

She added, "So, I asked the next old fellow sitting nearby if he also drank from the spring every day, to which he replied, 'I drink from the spring every day and I have milk in the morning, at noon and supper time.' And how old are you I asked?"

The old man replied, 'I'm 85.'

"Turning to the oldest looking man there I asked the same basic question and he answered, 'I drink from the spring every day and I have a woman in the morning, a woman at noon, and a woman in the evening every day,' in this frail voice.

"Somewhat surprised I asked, 'And how old are you?', to which he responded, "I'm 35."

FAO STUDY IN ROME

From Athens, we flew to Rome, where I reviewed the literature relevant to my project in the Food and Agriculture Organization (FAO) library for a six weeks period.

There was only one other American studying there that I knew of. That was Charlie Heck who was a forestry graduate student from Yale University. We had lunch together almost every day. One Sunday we went to the flea market along the Tigris River near the Vatican. It was very colorful and quite crowded. Charlie and I got separated for a while and when I ran into him later on, he was ecstatic with a big toothy smile.

He said, "Look at this, Stew", holding up a round coin.

I inspected it and didn't know anything about it.

Somewhat crestfallen Charlie said, "You don't realize what this is, do you?"

I replied, "You got that right. What is it?"

Charlie said, "It's a rare Eritrian coin."

"So what's the big deal about that? Why does that make you so happy?"

"Because, the stupid vendor did not realize how valuable this coin is and I got it for $2.00. It's got to be worth almost $20."

"So you certainly got the better of him then."

"Exactly, he just must not be very knowledgeable about how valuable it is."

Monday morning, I saw Charlie in the cafeteria line at FAO wearing a very glum face.

"Why so down in the mouth Charlie? You don't look too happy today," I said.

"Oh, that vendor cheated me yesterday. When I got home last night, I looked up the value of the Eritrian coin I bought and it isn't worth even a cotton pickin' dime."

"I hate to tell you this Charlie, but I really can't feel terrible sorry for your plight. Yesterday, you were so happy at the thought of screwing him and now it turns out that he screwed you." Charlie remained glum.

BALTIMORE

In Baltimore, I wrote up my studies and participated in the Master of Public Health (MPH) training program as a section head in the laboratory part of Pathobiology 1 course at the School of Hygiene and Public Health.

It was said that the only people on a permanent salary at Hopkins were the department heads and the janitors. Therefore, everyone else had to generate their own grants or they were unemployed.

After writing up most of my research for publication, I wrote a grant to return to India. The grant involved expanding my census and ecology work and included a study of Foot and Mouth Disease of cattle. My ecology section head, Chuck Southwick (an ecologist by training), said that I should delete the ecology part and emphasize the disease aspect. The head of the department, Fred Bang (a physician by training), said that I should forget the disease work and concentrate on the ecology study. Ironically, each was impressed with the area about which they had the least knowledge.

I never even submitted the grant paper to any granting agency. Interestingly, the grant was funded about 6 years later when I completed my PhD and it included both parts of the original grant.

MARRIAGE CRUMBLES

Bobbie and I were having some problems with our relationship. We went for marriage counseling at the American Family Services group every Wednesday night. The thing that I liked about this group was that one paid what one could afford. The cost varied from $2 to $25 per meeting per person depending upon their income tax status.

Before we started the group therapy sessions, I thought that there might be something wrong with me or Bobbie and she must have thought the same thing. However, when we heard the stories and complaints of the other couples in the group, we thought that we were uncommonly sane. Compared to their troubles, all of ours seemed trivial.

After about 6 months of attending the group therapy sessions, we announced that we had decided to get a divorce. All of the other participants were immediately saying that we were doing the wrong thing and attacked us verbally. The moderators (both male and female) explained that we had thought out everything and decided to do what we thought was in both our best interest. Further, the reason that the other folks were so anxious and upset was that such an action was very threatening to them. But they should not identify with our decision, as it really did not concern them and their particular problems.

1971

JOIN PFIZER, INC
In the spring of 1971 I took a job (50% increase in pay) with Charles Pfizer pharmaceutical company in Terre Haute, Indiana, as a research veterinarian. I liked the job a lot to begin with. I was working on producing the research which would allow new drugs to be cleared through the Food and Drug Administration (FDA).

I flew all over the country on a liberal expense account and set up drug trails at universities and other research institutions. I conducted experiments at our Terre Haute facility as well. However, I traveled about half time. After a while, I got tired of planes, motels, rental cars and unknown restaurants.

When I wanted to set up some experiments to answer some basic questions that had bearing on the work that we were doing, the administration blocked all basic research activities and intimated that if I was interested in that type of research I should take a job at a research university. They were only interested in applied research that helped get drugs on the market.

MARRIAGE NUMBER THREE
I had met a nurse in Baltimore (Nancy Hyre). One thing lead to another and she moved to Terre Haute, shortly after I did. We lived together in a house in the country and decided to get married after about 6 months. My mother and grandmother attended, as they had missed the other two marriages. Most of the guests were friends from Pfizer. Nancy's parents were Lutherans, so the marriage was performed in a Lutheran Church. Both Nancy and I were Unitarians but they had no minister in Terre Haute.

1972

INVITATION FROM THE UNIVERSITY OF CALIFORNIA AT DAVIS

Cal Schwabe the author of *Veterinary Medicine and Human Health* invited me to give a lecture in his course entitled "Perspectives on Veterinary Medicine" at the veterinary school in Davis, California. I arranged some research activity for Pfizer in Northern California at the same time. My mother came up for my talk and it was good to see old friends.

As I walked around the veterinary school I would see people that I recognized and walked up to them and said hi. I could figure out that they were a little confused as to who I was and I had to remind some of them. Others would recognize me and walk up to me and say hello, and ask where I had been, and I didn't have a clue who they were. I would apologetically ask their name.

After stumbling through several of such episodes, I decided to take the bull by the horns so to speak and be more assertive and aggressive. I saw this person who looked sort of familiar and I walked up to him and said, "Hey, it's good to see you again. I'm Stewart Odend'hal. I graduated in 1967; remember me?"

The guy had looked somewhat shocked when I had first walked up to him and he replied, "I only came here last year."

Oscar Schalm, the author of the text book, *Veterinary Hematology* came up to me and said, "Stew, I wish you would do me a big favor and join my group in pathology. You can work toward a PhD in comparative pathology or not. Just please yourself."

It was such a tempting offer and I felt embarrassed to turn him down. I had just been remarried and I liked my job in Terre Haute at that time and like an idiot, I wanted to be fair with Pfizer and not jump ship. As I look back on this opportunity, my rejection of this offer was one of my biggest mistakes in my life.

DECIDED TO LEAVE PFIZER

One day I was working on an experimental trial for a new drug at the Terre Haute Federal penitentiary farm and drove back to the office to get my peanut butter and banana sandwich which I had forgotten.

When I walked in the office, one of the secretaries said, "Dr. Odend'hal, you are supposed to be in the auditorium for the big meeting right now."

I said, "What big meeting? No one told me anything about a meeting today."

She replied, "Apparently, it was called at the last minute. The vice-president from New York is presenting some new assignments or something."

So, I dutifully ran into the auditorium, as this stranger from New York was saying, "So as you can see from the charts, we are having a completely new emphasis in this regard."

"What regard?" I said silently to myself.

Then he called out the new assignments, "And Odend'hal, you will now be in the central research arena and answer to Groton, Connecticut." He continued on with the reassignments for the other 12 professional employees that were present.

Later on I said to a colleague, "I never heard of Groton, Connecticut. What the hell is there?"

"That's where all of the new drugs are developed. They test them on rats and mice and now it looks like we will be the ones to design and test the drugs in the animal species for which they are intended to be used for various indications."

At the end of the meeting, the vice-president explained that the corporate jet would be here tomorrow to take those of us who would be working with the central research group to Groton.

We spent three days there being wined and dined and toured the research facility. The last night we had this big dinner at the country club to celebrate our attachment to our new assignments. Various administrators picked up each of us newcomers and took us separately to the affair. My host was the man who was in charge of all animal research for the North American continent.

113

I told him, "You know, I am glad that I am now in central research instead of developmental research, but I am not too happy the way we had no say so at all and it was sort of rammed down our throats. How long did you know that this major shift was going to take place?"

His answer totally startled me. He said, "I had no idea or fore warning. I found out the same day that you all did in Terre Haute."

I thought at that time, that I would extricate myself from Pfizer. If a man with a new appointment to a higher position in New York, could look at a chart and just move people around without so much as a courtesy contact to those involved, then I'm out of here. I felt like a leaf upon the sea to be carried here and there with no choice of my own. I did not want some unknown person to direct my life. I should have called Oscar Schalm and taken him up on his offer, but that thought never occurred to me until just this moment (June 20, 2009) [What a dummy I am].

I just remembered why I did not contact Dr. Schalm. When I told my wife that I was going to quit Pfizer and go back to graduate school, she made the following request. She said that if I was going to graduate school, she would like to have it at a school that also had a nursing graduate program that she might be able to enter if she wanted to do so. The University of California at Davis did not have such a nursing program at that time. So, I don't feel so dumb anymore; just sorry about my defective and aging memory chip.

1973

UNIVERSITY OF ILLINOIS FIASCO

I began in earnest to locate graduate school programs with appeal. I went one week end at the veterinary school in Illinois. The graduate recruiter showed me a new computer program that they were developing.

I sat down in front of the computer that was loaded with a software program to sharpen diagnostic skills. The first case was of a dog with a bent neck as the only presenting sign. After answering several

114

questions, I turned to the recruiter and said, "It would sure help if I could see the dog."

He answered, "Go ahead; ask to see the dog."

I laughed and said, "That's ridiculous. How can I possibly see the dog?"

"Go ahead and ask. What do you have to lose?"

So, lo and behold, when I typed that I would like to see the dog, a clear color photograph appeared on the monitor of the dog. When I asked to see the x-ray; a radiograph appeared on the screen.

This software development was called Plato and was marvelous for its time. I decided that I did not want to join the Illinois program for a variety of reasons.

About a week later, my boss, George Thrasher, asked me to go with him to the Illinois veterinary school to talk with a veterinarian who had perfected a method to produce germ-free piglets. After our interview with the veterinarian, we were walking down the hall and I saw this same computer and suggested that we go into the room and see what this computer had to offer.

George was slightly reluctant, because he said that we should head back to Terre Haute. I insisted and we went in and I told George that I had read about this software and he should try his hand at a diagnosis.

After he was into the program and was somewhat perplexed, I said, "Why don't you ask to see the dog?"

George responded, "God, you're funny Odend'hal."

"No, seriously; ask to see the dog. Let's see what might happen."

"Why should I do something that is an exercise in futility?"

"What have you got to lose?" I countered.

"Valuable time; I want to hit the road to Terre Haute."

"Just try it once," I pleaded.

"Okay, but this is just to get you to shut up."

Trying to hide the smirk on my face, I watched as George typed in, "I want to see the dog."

To my great consternation, absolutely nothing happened. The screen turned blank.

George looked at me with that, "I told you so" look, shaded with a touch of disgust.

"Huh, come on George, try it again" I suggested trying to calm my composure.

"What the hell's wrong with you Odend'hal? I'm going back to Terre Haute. You can stay here with your fantasies and take a bus back if you don't want to go now." He was clearly losing his patience.

With my tail between my legs, I followed him out the door. I just couldn't bring myself to tell him that I had seen it before. I was frightened that he would have wanted to know what I was doing there before. I didn't want to let him know I was thinking about leaving Pfizer and suffer a premature expulsion.

Later on, I talked with someone from Illinois and told them of my ordeal and asked what had happened to the Plato program. He said that it just had good days and bad days and sometimes it worked and sometimes it didn't. It was just my unlucky day.

THE SKY'S APPEARANCE DEPENDS ON WHO IS LOOKING AT IT

One week while working for Pfizer I flew around the country to set up experimental trials to test a new anthelmintic (a worm killing agent) for cattle. One day I finished up my contacts, checked out of my motel room in Lafayette, Louisiana and drove to the airport in my rental car.

116

The sky was half full of puffy white cumulus clouds. The weather forecaster on the radio stated that today the sky was partially sunny.

After landing in Amarillo, Texas, I was driving to my motel in my rental car and I noticed that the sky had exactly the same appearance as that in Lafayette, i.e. it was half full of white puffy cumulus clouds. When I turned on the radio, I heard the weatherman say that in Amarillo, the sky was partly cloudy.

I deduced from this experience that they wanted the sun in rain soaked Lafayette and they wanted the clouds in bone dry Amarillo. They say that the average yearly rainfall in Amarillo is 10 inches. If you look back at the yearly statistics, one can see that they had 20 inches one year and only 1 inch in the next year. But statistically that worked out to be an average of 10 inches per year.

START GRADUATE SCHOOL AT
THE UNIVERSITY OF MISSOURI
In the summer I gave Pfizer a month's notice, resigned and started graduate school at the School of Veterinary Medicine at the University of Missouri at Columbia, Missouri. I was classified as a research associate, was paid $14,000 per year and was able to work toward my PhD in veterinary anatomy/immunology. I had saved up $7,000 and put that amount down on the purchase of a $30,000 house in Columbia.

1974

I BLATANTLY BREAK THE LAW
In January, one of the locals told me not to forget to buy a "city sticker". In order to drive on the city streets of Columbia, Missouri, your car had to display a little decal in the upper left hand corner of the windshield. If the cops saw that you did not have a city sticker (a terrible method to raise taxes for the city), then you got a substantial fine.

I heard that I had to go to the city hall to buy the city sticker, so there I went and stood in a long line for about 30 minutes. When I got to the window, the lady said, "Can I see your title and registration?"

I replied, "I don't have it."

She said, "I can't serve you until you have it."

"Okay, I'll go get it and come back."

So a couple of days later I again got into the line, which was even longer than the first time I attempted to buy the city sticker. After a comparable wait, I reached the front of the line and made my request to buy a city sticker. But this time I was informed that I needed to have my insurance paper with me as well as the title and registration papers.

Irate that the first person did not tell me about this, I left the city hall in a huff. I had heard that if you have paid for a city sticker in another city in Missouri, then you did not have to buy one in Columbia. So I thought, "to heck with them at the Columbia city hall.", and I refused to go back a third time.

Then for four years, every time I saw a cop car, I would immediately revise my path and turn off before I got near. I never got caught, and I never felt guilty of my act of civil disobedience. Before or since, I have never lived anywhere they collected taxes by that method.

1975

NOBEL LAUREATE TYPE SPEAKERS

There were two Nobel laureate type speakers that I heard at Missouri: Hans Selye, and Hans Krebs. Also, I heard Buckminster Fuller (who should have been a Nobel laureate).

Hans Selye, who was the first person to describe the General Adaptive Syndrome (Stress) spoke about stress. He said what was stressful for one person was not necessarily stressful to another. He said that there were only two basic types of human beings; race horses and turtles. Take a race horse and stick him on the beach at Miami and that would be terribly stressful to him. Take the turtle and stick him there and he would be in paradise.

Hans Krebs, spoke and was one of the most boring speakers I have ever heard. It wasn't so much that I could not understand him; his monotone delivery and lack of enthusiasm was not pleasant. His central message was that the tricarboxylic acid cycle had such a wide application to all of physiology.

Buckminster Fuller was far and away the most entertaining and gave an enlightening talk. I do not remember what outstanding points he presented, but the enthusiasm and humor was very enjoyable. The auditorium was completely packed with both aisles crammed with people (it was a fire marshal's nightmare). At one point, as he was gesticulating with his hands, he stopped talking and held his right hand up above his head and stared at his right hand that was wiggling. After a pregnant pause, he looked at the audience and said, "Just look at that hand. It's over 83 years old and still works perfectly."

TRIP TO AUSTRALIA
I never really remember meeting my father until I was 15 years old. I decided that I wanted to see my son, Phil, before he was 15, so I went to Australia while he was still in the tender age of 13.

Due to my mother's advice I was able to get a "Fly-Drive Package" that included, a roundtrip plane ticket (LA – Sydney); 3 weeks motel stay; and a rental car for the three weeks with a credit for 500 free miles of driving. This package was only 70% of the cost just for an airplane round trip ticket between LA and Sydney. My mother owned a travel agency in Laguna Beach. She specialized in cruises and other types of trips. However, she absolutely refused to deal with airline tickets in any way. She said that they were constantly changing and did not make any sense and were too complicated to book, etc. As I write this some 25 years later, I understand her frustration completely.

I took Phil and his slightly disturbed younger brother to fairs, on glider rides, to the Sydney opera house and in general had a delightful time. My ex-wife intimated that she wanted to get back together again. However, I found that prospect unappealing.

Phil was good at soccer and his teammates called him "Hollywood", since he was born there.

BICYCLE RIDING

I used to ride my bicycle about 8 miles to and from school every day. On one of the returning roads in the evening, there was always a very long line of cars waiting for one particular traffic light to change. It was just a single lane of cars and I used to despise that situation. Here I was using a nonpolluting method of transportation and I had to breathe all of the exhaust fumes from those stagnant autos.

On one unforgettable journey home, as I was passing everyone on the right side of their vehicles, a lady, frustrated with the delay suddenly opened the back door of a car and I had to sharply turn to the right to avoid hitting her or the car door. Luckily, I was able to keep control and not go careening off into the bushes along the road.

One week end, I talked my wife, Nancy, into taking a 20 mile bike ride over to the Missouri river along interstate 70. Everything went great to get to the river; however, on the way back, the frontage road that paralleled the interstate had been freshly covered with small sized gravel and black gooey tar. As we cycled along, we both became aware of the fact that pumping the petals became more and more difficult. The black tar and gravel slowly built up on the surface of the tires and pressed against the fenders of the bike. Before long, we could not even make the tires turn as the tires were completely and solidly jammed against the fenders. Unfortunately, we had no choice but to walk for several miles before we came to a place that we could call friends to come and get us.

STUDENT'S REVENGE

There was one professor of physiology that almost all of the students disliked. He was an ex-army veterinarian who was rigid, humorless and very unforgiving. When he went down the aisle to collect the tests papers after giving an exam, if one person in the row did not hand his or her paper to the person sitting next to the aisle in time, the professor would not accept it and every person in that row would receive a zero grade for that particular quiz.

He lived across a wide creek just to the east of the veterinary school. He would walk across a large wide sewer pipe over the creek about 6 feet above the bottom of the ravine. Usually, he took his prized female Labrador with him to school.

One day, the students greased the pipe. As the dog trotted in front of the professor, all of a sudden the dog slipped and fell off of the pipe. As the professor explained to me later, he thought to himself at the time, that the dog was just stupid and clumsy. Then he added, the next thing he knew he was also at the bottom of the creek.

He loved his dog for another reason. She was a cash cow, in that she whelped lots of pure breed puppies that he sold to supplement his income. Whenever he would go out of town for any reason, he would board the dog at the veterinary school. When some of the older students found out that his dog was there at the veterinary school they played a mean trick. They anesthetized the dog, made a midline ventral surgical incision usually done for a spay (ovariohysterectomy) and sutured it up without entering the abdominal cavity.

When the good doctor came back from his trip he was told very apologetically, that a terrible error had been made. He was told that his beloved Labrador had been spayed by mistake, thinking it was a client's dog. There was nothing amusing or satisfying with his response.

"SPAY EVERY DOG AND CAT IN COLUMBIA"
I was the president of the Central Missouri Human Society in Columbia. We were having a fund raising drive to replace the old humane society shelter with a new one and we received lots of publicity in the local media.

We had been awarded a $50,000 grant from the American Humane Association and I was successful in getting matching funds from the city government. But we still needed more money. I went to talk with the vice-president of the largest bank about a loan to complete the new shelter if we did not raise enough during the drive. He agreed and also was kind enough to put a small note into the monthly statements of all of their customers advising then to donate to the new shelter.

Toward the end of the fund raising drive I stopped by the shelter and as I walked in the front door, the shelter manager said, "Here he is right now. You can talk to him." As he handed me the phone, I asked him who was on the phone and he indicated that he had no idea.

An abbreviated transcript would go something like the following:

"Hello."

"Are you the president?"

"Yes."

"I want to donate some money to the humane society."

"Great, we really can use the money for the new shelter."

"I don't want it to go to the new shelter."

"Oh, that's fine. We can always use donations to defray our operating expenses which are considerable."

"I don't want it to go to the operating expenses."

"Then what do you want the money to go towards?"

"Can you meet me at the country club at noon next Tuesday for lunch?"

"Yes, I think I can."

"It's settled then. I will see you there next Tuesday. Ask to be seated at Smith's table. And, oh yeah, bring along your vice-president, Mr. Jenkins."

"Mr. Jenkins is not our vice-president. He is the vice-president of the bank."

"Bring him along anyway. Good-bye."

So, I called Mr. Jenkins, asked if he could join me for lunch and enquired as to who Smith was. He indicated that he had no idea at all, but that he would be there for lunch.

At 11:55 am Mr. Jenkins and I walked into the country club and asked to be shown to Mr. Smith's table for lunch. Sitting at the table was a very small skinny man who looked to be around 65 to 70 years old.

We introduced ourselves and we sat down. I asked what this was all about and he said, "Let's wait until my wife gets here."

So, we waited and within a short time of silence, Mr. Smith's wife appeared. She turned out to be an imposing sight. She was quite tall, heavy set, wearing tasteful expensive clothes and a bee hive hairdo. She also had lots of jewelry.

She sat down and began talking immediately. "Which one of you is Dr. Odend'hal?"

After she knew who I was, she looked directly at me and said, "Last year I was diagnosed with cancer. I thought I was going to die. Now it looks like I will not die. But upon reflection of that possibility, I said to myself, I want to do something that will make a difference. So I, er we, want to give you a substantial amount of money so that you can spay and neuter all of the dogs and cats in the city of Columbia."

I explained that it was a noble endeavor, but destined to fail in the long run, since Columbia was a university town with new students bringing in new pets every year.

At that juncture, Mr. Jenkins, then made a blatant attempt to snatch the money for his bank; touting their city development fund for civic improvement.

Wrestling the focus of attention back to the humane society situation, I was finally successful in making the following proposal. We would graciously accept their donation with the money going to pay for the spaying and neutering of all animals adopted out from the shelter for one year. We would keep accurate records of the use of that money and they could examine the records at the end of one year. If they were

123

dissatisfied with the results, we would return the money from the next year's budget.

They agreed, but they did not want any publicity of their donation. However, we could announce it without using their name. They in essence gave the humane society stock in Mr. Smith's company on December 30th and sold the stock, giving us the money from that sale in February. What was stated as a $20,000 donation in December turned out to be worth over $28,000 in February. At the end of the first year, everybody involved was happy (including the animals).

When I left for India a year later, we dedicated the new shelter.

1977

MARRIAGE NUMBER THREE CRUMBLES

Toward the end of my PhD studies, as I sat down at the breakfast table, my wife said nonchalantly, "Do you want to come with me to the lawyer's office at 2 pm today or not?"

"Why are you going to see a lawyer today?"

"Because I'm getting a divorce," she responded.

"What! Are you kidding me? I never heard anything about a divorce until today," was my outburst.

"Well, I knew you wouldn't like it, so I did it all on my own."

I do not remember whether it was shortly before this or after this that she stayed away all night. So, I knew that she was unfaithful. Although, I was very angry at the lawyer's office that afternoon, I agreed to the divorce without any real trouble or resistance.

That afternoon following the visit to the lawyer's office Nancy said, "I want you to move out."

I said, "Me move out? You move out. I bought the house and pay the mortgage. This whole idea is your doing, so you move out."

Nancy rented a mobile home in a trailer park where her best friend, Lin, lived on the south side of Columbia. My colleague, who lived nearby, always referred to the trailer park mobile homes as, "That place with all of the tool sheds".

After Nancy had done all of the leg work and rented the place, I told her that I would move out and she could stay in the house. She had two dogs and there was no place to keep them at the mobile home park. Our house also had a fenced-in back yard.

SEARCHING FOR A JOB

I had applied for a grant from the Indo-US Subcommission on Education and Culture. I wanted to reinvestigate the same two study sites that I had surveyed in 1967-1970 and also determine if Indian squirrels might have a role in the transmission of Foot and Mouth Disease (FMD). I was placed on an alternate list and informed that I had two chances to be awarded the grant, i.e. slim and none.

I answered an advertisement for a histology instructor at the School of Veterinary Medicine at the University of Georgia in Athens, Georgia. The day before I left to go down to Georgia for the interview, I received the announcement that I had indeed received the grant from the Indo-US Subcommission to go the India for 10 months.

Therefore, at the conclusion of my interview in Georgia, I weighed the prospects of the two positions and told them that I had decided to take the grant and go to India, but that I appreciated the offer, but would have to decline. To my utter amazement, the Georgia folks had a short conference and asked if I would accept their offer when I returned. If I agreed, they would make adjustments in their teaching. This was an offer that I could not refuse. To try and find a job while living in India seemed problematic. With an assured position at Georgia, I could concentrate on my work in India more effectively.

MARRIAGE NUMBER FOUR BEGINS

Although I knew that Nancy's best friend, Lin McNickle, lived at the same trailer park, I made no effort to search her out and did not even look out for her. Then one night, Dr. Dey, a Bengali veterinarian asked me to go to a guitar recital and I reluctantly agreed. When we sat down in our seats, I felt a tap on my shoulder and Lin was sitting directly behind us. I asked for her to join us in our row.

One thing led to another and we lived together for the last month or so while I finished up my PhD. I did not want to get married. After all, I was a three time loser. However, I thought it would be great if Lin would come with me to India. She wanted to and the financial situation turned out to be an important factor.

If we did not get married and she came with me, I would have to pay about $2,000 for her round trip airline ticket and easily another $1,000 for her maintenance in India. If we got married, the grant would pay all of these expenses. So, it was a question of $6,000 difference and I could not even afford to pay for her airline ticket. The issue became a no-brainer and we were married on a friend's farm outside of town a week or so before we left for India.

EXCISED MEDIAL MENISCUS

One month before we left for India I played a fairly heated tennis match with Jim Koukl, my best friend in Columbia. Afterward I went over to the library at the veterinary school and was talking with Trenton Boyd, the librarian. I put my head on the desk and spread my legs putting more than usual pressure on my medial meniscus which is the crescent shaped fibrocartilage which fills the space between my patella (knee cap) and the surrounding bones.

Immediately after I left the library, I thought to myself, 'I've got to hurry back home to catch the evening news.' As I picked up speed, suddenly I heard a crack and intense pain flooded my left knee.

The doctor (a veterinarian, who went back to medical school and became an orthopedic surgeon) explained that I could be in big trouble if the broken cartilage tore loose in village India. So I agreed to have it removed. At my request, the anesthesiologist gave me a spinal so that I could watch the procedure. However, with the surgical incision I said, "I feel that." And immediately, I was out as the anesthesiologist injected a powerful anesthetic into the intravenous drip.

After I had my cast removed I was on crutches for a while. Lin and I went to Kansas City to a nice restaurant. When we came out and I was searching for the keys to the car in my pocket, I heard a noise that sounded like a metal object hitting the pavement nearby. Acknowledging the sound but not investigating it, I started to get into the car.

When I put all of my weight on the crutch handle bar, there was no resistance whatsoever and I went crashing to the ground. Lying next to me on the ground was the wing nut and steel pin that secured the handle bar to the rest of the crutch. I learned from this experience, that when something unusual happens, it is always best to investigate immediately instead of just ignoring it. I say, I learned, but actually I didn't, because I have made the same mistake many times over. Maybe in my eighties I will become more observant.

ARRIVAL IN INDIA AND CUSTOMS

As an Indian friend once observed, "Indian customs officials are like tigers waiting to pounce upon the unsuspecting new arrivals." I laughed at the time, not anticipating that I would become one of their unfortunate victims.

When we arrived in Delhi and the customs officer expressed an unusual interest in Lin's guitar, I smugly mentioned to her that I was sure I could handle any problem. No problem developed, as the guitar was passed. Then the officer looked at the large card board box containing 500 Petri dishes and asked, "What is this?"

I explained that I was doing some immunological tests that required plastic Petri dishes and that they were not available in India and I could not do the research with glass Petri dishes which was all that they had available here in India.

"You cannot bring these dishes into India without an exemption to do so."

"Where do I obtain such an exemption?"

"You can obtain an exemption from the University Grants Commission."

"Where is the University Grants Commission and who do I see there?"

At this point, the subcommission host who met us at the airport said that he could arrange everything. It was merely a minor technicality and we should enjoy a day or so of sightseeing; thus, started an eight day farce.

When our host dropped us off at the YWCA hotel near Connaught Circle, I noticed that the headlines of the English language newspaper said, "90,000 new cases of malaria in the Delhi area". Immediately, I went to the nearest pharmacy and bought lots of quinine tablets and Lin and I started taking the drug.

The next day our host arrived with triumphant news that tomorrow we would get the valued exemption notice. After the third day of such an announcement our host explained that the deputy of the University Grants Commission was in the hospital with malaria.

"Can't the vice-deputy sign an exemption?" I asked.

"Oh, no. That could never happen. We must wait until the deputy is released from the hospital." he replied.

"What if he died? Then couldn't the vice-deputy sign it?"

"Yes, of course, but since the deputy is still alive, he cannot sign it."

"That seems rather stupid to me."

"Nevertheless, that is just the way it is, I am afraid." was his response.

A similar exchange occurred for the next two days. In desperation, we took an all day trip to see the Taj Mahal in the city of Agra about a 4 hour train ride southeast of Delhi. Upon our return, it was another couple of days before the host arrived one day with the belated exemption notice.

As we were driving to the airport to collect the Petri dishes, I asked to see the exemption. The exemption said that I would not sell the Petri dishes. Further, the exemption stated that I would take them back to the United States upon my departure from India.

When I saw this, I told the host that I could not take the Petri dishes back to the U.S. as they would be contaminated with FMD viruses. He blithely said, "Don't worry about that statement. It is a minor technicality of no concern to the customs officer." Silently questioning the veracity of his statement, the taxi he had hired careened along the Delhi streets toward the airport.

In those days, if anyone spent at least 2 hours in a customs arena in an Indian airport, there would be one passenger, who would lose control and explode in frustration with an outburst that attracted everyone's attention. This was my day to explode.

The custom officer read the exemption and told me to follow him to the baggage room, where questionable items were stored. He presented me with a bill for storage for a fairly large sum of rupees. I resisted payment and argued with him for some time. I truly have repressed the outcome and do not remember whether or not I paid, or refused.

After this altercation and I had the box of Petri dishes in my hand we went over to the exit door and as I remember, he then asked me to sign the statement that I would take all of the Petri dishes back to the US when I left the country.

I tried to explain that such thing was impossible, as I would be the ultimate most irresponsible person on earth if I spread FMD virus all over the world. He was insistent. I exploded and hollered and ranted and raved. My host, was saying, "Calm down, he is going to let you bring the Petri dishes into India."

I barely heard him as I was by that time oblivious to anyone stopping me from having my say. I said to the custom agent that if he insisted on such a ridiculous request, I would bring all of the infected Petri dishes back to his house and dump them all over his house.

By that time a crowd had gathered and the custom agent's eyes were very big and he was obviously angry. I didn't care and was very hard to calm down. The host was saying something to the agent in Hindi and I just grabbed the box of Petri dishes and walked out.

RESILIENCY OF LIFE IN INDIA

When I was in India for two and a half years between 1967 and 1970, I noticed a very attractive young lady who lived on the sidewalk near Howrah train station next to where people waited for taxis. She always had the most pleasant expression on her face and she interacted with those around her in such a nice way. One time late in the evening I thought I saw her with her husband. He looked like a Rajastani because of his red turban and he probably worked as a baggage handler.

I looked for her every time I went through Howrah station and finally one day I caught a glimpse of her across the sidewalk where she used to be 10 years before. I walked over to her and spoke to her in Bengali. She had aged tremendously. She said that she had 5 kids, all born right there on the sidewalk and had been living there continuously. After I knew where to look for her, every time I came through Howrah I would see if I could see her. And just like 10 years before, she was obviously a very pleasant person and interacted with those around her so nicely.

I thought here is a person, who most westerners would feel sorry for. She did not have a roof over her head. She had to go far to get water to cook her meals for her family. The opportunity for her kids must seem extremely constricted. Yet, here she was, not feeling sorry for herself or her family and doing the best she could under the circumstances. She was and hopefully still is a beautiful person. Truly the resiliency of life in India is amazing.

MY FIRST WIFE COMMITS SUICIDE IN AUSTRALIA

I had only been in India for about three weeks. After completing a work day in the villages, I was waiting for the train on the platform of Singur station. A man that I did not know came up to me and said that I should go to the All India Institute of Hygiene and Public Health Rural Training Center immediately, but did not say why.

I followed him into a large room with many people sitting at desks and allegedly working. I could see that there was an air of anticipation and everyone was looking at me out of the corner of their eyes. They asked me to sit down, which I did. Then another stranger came up to me and said, "We have received a telegram for you. I will read it to you."

He read the telegram in a very loud voice, so that all in the room could hear it. The telegram said that Gail Odend'hal had committed suicide and I should go to Australia at once. The telegram had been sent by my mother. I was totally devastated and began to sob immediately. No one moved. They all just sat there and stared. I could not stop crying. I hated the inconsiderate nature of this announcement to the whole room and nowhere to seek solitude. It left a bitter feeling toward the people who live there.

I made arrangements to fly to Sydney the next day and spent 5 days there. I found out that Gail had gone to several doctors and each had written her a prescription for valium. Her best friend told me that Gail had planned everything. She made a will. She got drunk, took as much of the valium she could hold and then went out and drove the car off of a cliff. She died instantly, as far as I know.

My son, Phil was 15 years old. His half-brother, Brett was 11 years old. Gail's live-in boyfriend said that he would care for the boys. I tried to get the boys to come back with me to India and put them both in a private school in Calcutta, but they both refused. Phil said that he was dropping out of school and would get a job. I urged him to continue in school. I asked him, out of his ten best friends how many were not continuing school and he said at least 8 were not continuing in school.

Reluctantly, I returned to India without them. I talked with his grandfather who was in a nursing home. He said that he would keep in touch about the welfare of the kids.

The most amazing aspect of the trip to Australia was the following. I loved Gail and was so sad that she had died. In Sydney, on at least three or four occasions, I saw a blonde woman with a similar figure. I wished so badly that she was not dead that I ran after them because I was sure that she was not dead and I could find her alive. It probably was a little like the situation when Jesus died, or Elvis. People wanted

131

them to both be alive so strongly that they were sure that they saw them.

Each time it happened, I also was convinced that the woman was Gail until I walked directly in front of the woman and determined that she was not Gail. It was slightly embarrassing on a couple of occasions, but the desire was so compulsive, I could not stop.

1978

It would be impossible to capture every interesting and significant event that occurred in India over a ten month period. Suffice to say that every week something happened that was a surprise.

A USUAL ROUTINE DAY

I would wake up about 4:00 am, eat a quick breakfast and go out to catch a street car about 6 blocks from my apartment. The streetcar would carry me to Howrah train station across the Hooghly River from Calcutta. I would catch a train to my study site of Singur around 6 am and arrive there around 7 am. My field workers would meet me there and we would ride our bicycles to a study village around 8 am. We would work until 12:00 noon and then ride back to Singur and I would take the train back to Calcutta, arriving back at my apartment around 3 pm.

After six months in the Singur area, we moved to Jhalda in Purulia district. It was an overnight train ride from Calcutta to Jhalda which is near the border of the state of Bihar. We were there for four months and had an easier schedule. Up at 6 am, walk to the field station (2.5 miles), accumulate the necessary equipment and drive to the villages and work there from 8 am until noon. Back at the field station, we would record the data and stop work around 3 or 4 pm.

AMERICAN RED TAPE

I had a $7,000 supplementary grant for the National Science Foundation. I had met some other grant recipients in Calcutta who were buying up rugs and art to ship back to the USA when their grant had ended with their left over funds. I disapproved of such behavior (I don't like "things" anyway) so I decided to return the unused portion of my grant money which consisted of about $1,500 as I remember.

When I went to the American embassy, the science attaché was perplexed, because he did not know how to accept the money back.

After three days going back and forth, he finally figured out how to accept the money, but it cost me several days of living expenses in Delhi, which I thought was really unnecessary.

An amusing side light to this ordeal, was the realization that if you used the stairs instead of the elevators in the embassy, you could tell who was new to India and who was a seasoned veteran of living in India. As you would come down or go up the stairs and came to a landing in between floors, if you passed another American at that landing, the newcomers would go to the right, while the people who had been living in India always started to pass on the left. This was because of the fact that people in the US are used to passing on the right and in India they pass on the left. Occasionally, you would actually bump into the other American, if they were new arrivals to India.

GIN-GIN AND SHUKIE WORLD TRAVELERS

Like naïve idiots we decided to ship our Indian cat (Gin-gin) and Indian dog (Shukie) back to the USA. The story of the trials and tribulations could fill a book.

Lin said, "I want to take Gin-gin back to the USA with us."

I said, "No way, Jose. That would be extremely time consuming and terribly expensive."

Lin said, "I really mean it. Gin-gin will die here if we don't take her back."

"Well, in that case, I want to take Shukie back with us also." I said this just to show how ridiculous such ideas were.

Lin said, "Okay." So that's what we did.

The packers had constructed a huge cage for Shukie. When we arrived in Delhi around midnight I traced down the whereabouts of the cargo area and heard this piercing cry of Shukie, whose head was sticking out of the wire window that he had chewed through. For about 2 hours I searched around to obtain a hammer and nails to try and fix the wire window, so Shukie could not escape on the way back.

Shukie and Gin-gin flew back via Los Angeles and Lin and I via London. By the time that the animals reached LA, the Human Society there bought Shukie a new cage, as he had demolished his cage. We paid for it later.

ON TO ATHENS, GEORGIA

We flew back to Columbia, Missouri to pick up our stuff. My ex-wife, Nancy wanted me to sign over the house to her, which I did. When we met at the savings and loan office, she said that she "knew" that I had been unfaithful to her by sleeping with Lin. I found her accusation so wildly untrue; I just laughed and told her to go ask Lin who was across the lobby from where we were sitting.

Apparently, she did go tell Lin that was what she thought and it pissed Lin off, because they were best friends and Lin was offended. Ironically, I was not the unfaithful one, but Nancy was for sure. I don't know if Nancy felt guilty about her infidelity and decided to delude herself to protect her ego, or what. Unfortunately, the little guy that she fell in love with (who reminded me exactly of her father) beat her up. He turned out to be a drug addict and almost blinded her in one eye.

I bought a Datsun 210 from the father-in-law of one of the veterinary students and we drove to Nebraska to pick up Shukie and Gin-gin from Lin's mother in the little town of Farnum, Nebraska. Amazingly, at her mother's there was a local newspaper from the next town, Curtis, which had a picture of the veterinary student from Missouri, whose father-in-law sold me the car in Columbia.

I went over to Curtis to the veterinary practice where he was serving as an apprentice and talked to him. He told me that his father-in-law was an alcoholic and sold me the car way under the regular price because I knew him.

Another remarkable thing happened while staying in Farnum. I went to see my brother, Charles in Boulder, Colorado, a day's drive away. I was so sick with stomach pain, diarrhea and listlessness I went to see a gastroenterologist. He said that he was almost certain that I was suffering from an infestation of Giardia lambria, an intestinal parasite that is often misdiagnosed by general practitioners. He could treat me with a giardiacide and if I got better, then most likely the presumptive diagnosis would be correct. Otherwise to make an accurate diagnosis, he would have to put me in the hospital, stick a tube down into the duodenum and sample the digestive juices to actually see the giardia. Rectal sampling is always negative as the parasite is destroyed toward the end of the alimentary tract.

Sure enough, all of my signs and symptoms disappeared and I made a complete recovery. Every time I went to India, I didn't have any trouble with giardia, that I know of. However, every times I came back and ate good rich nutritious food, giardia would flare up and I would each time be miserable until I took the medication of a giardiacide.

IN ATHENS, GEORGIA

You may laugh, but my Indian dog barked with an accent. The other dogs could tell he was a foreigner. His bark was like most dogs, except it also had a raspy sound at the same time. So, it ended up sort of sounding like a bark and a howl at the same time.

At first we rented a duplex. We were just looking around to get ideas about building a house, but fell in love with this house in the tiny town of Watkinsville, GA. There were two acres (one of which was a swamp next to a perennial creek). It had three bedrooms, with floor to ceiling windows in the living room. There was a huge deck that over looked the swamp and the eaves were so wide that you could leave the windows open when it rained. There were so many trees that we never could see our neighbors in the summer time. An amusing coincidence was the fact that my car model was a Datsun 210. My address was 210 Colliers Creek road and my office address was number 210. A statistician would go wild.

1979

A PUBLICATION THWARTED

Conscious of the "publish or perish" dictates of a scientific academic career, I was always looking out for significant opportunities to publish a research note or two. Very early one morning as I looked out with contentment over my humble acreage, I suddenly spied an opossum with what appeared to be a huge tumor. The opossum was dragging its belly with obvious difficulty in our fenced-in back yard.

Quick as a wink, I had picked up a large card board box and ran into the back yard to capture the opossum. My intent was to surgically remove the tumor and characterize the type and thus obtain accolades from my colleagues and even perhaps describe a newly undiscovered tumor.

As I chased the opossum around the yard, the opossum eventually was cornered where the back and side fences met. I picked up the box and was just about to place it over the opossum, when she raised up her body and what should I see, but a bunch of tiny tails wiggling out of the opening of her pouch. No tumor there, but just a bunch of baby opossums. Even though I was slightly disappointed that I had just lost a possible publication, I was happy that she didn't have a tumor and she was free to go on her way.

SOME OF SHUKIE'S EXCAPADES

It was amazing to me that every November Shukie would go roaming. This coincided with the breeding season back in India. It seemed an innate response to perhaps reduce the chance of inbreeding. If the male dogs got a wander lust when the females were entering heat, there would be less likelihood of breeding with close relatives.

There appeared to be only one heat period in Indian dogs, as puppies were only born around January and February of each year. This was the time of year that the pups had the greatest chance for survival.

At any rate, Shukie would go roaming in November. I allowed him to run loose all of the time anyway, but in November he might be gone for several days or up to a week and not be seen. One year, Shukie showed up with a piece of paper attached to his collar. When I opened it up, the note said, "If you own this dog, call this number". By the telephone number, I knew that it was nearby.

So, I called the number. A lady answered the phone and I told her that I got the note and was responding as requested. She said that she was glad that there was an owner and they liked the dog. I asked, "Is he bothering you at all?" ; to which she replied, "I'd better let you talk with my husband."

Her husband explained that they liked the dog and what was his name. I said, "Shukie. He is an Indian dog and Shukie means happiness in Bengali."

He was immediately full of excitement and said, "Ellen, come here, come here. The dog's name is Shukie which means happiness in Bengali." Then he went on to explain to me that they didn't know what to call the dog, so they called him Happy, because he seemed so happy.

When I asked him if Shukie was bothering them, he said, "Now don't get me wrong because we like your dog as I said. But we have a dog and we love our dog. We feed our dog in the garage and leave the garage door open most of the time. Your dog comes in and eats our dog's dog food and will not let our dog near his own food. I like your dog so much, I thought well we will just adopt him and feed him separately. But now that I know that he is an owned dog, it might be better if you would keep your dog at your place and keep him on a leash."

I acknowledged that I would do that. About a month after the phone call and I had started to keep Shukie on a leash, I was walking him around the neighborhood. Another neighbor was having a garage sale and had tricycles, wagons, mowers and other larger implements lined on either side of his long driveway. Because this neighbor was a friend of mine that also worked at the veterinary school I was walking up the driveway to say hi.

The lady of an elderly couple also walking up the driveway said, "Look Fred, there's Shukie." As I turned around to see who they were, Shukie lifted his evil leg and peed all over the tricycle and wagon. Yanking Shukie vigorously away from the drenched items, I pulled the leach tightly and brought the mischievous dog next to me. As Fred and Ellen approached, they said that they were the ones who sent the note on his collar a couple of months ago. I relaxed the leash. When Ellen stood right in front of me wearing an expensive very nice cream colored cashmere sweater, Shukie recognized her and immediately jumped up to greet her. Unfortunately, he had very dark red muddy paws, which he planted firmly upon her significantly endowed breasts.

"Oh Fred, look what he's done." she screamed.

Pulling Shukie away with a firm jerk, I said, "Oh my gosh, I'm so sorry. I gotta run."

1980

FOUR MONTHS IN HAITI

African Swine Fever (ASF) virus infections had been diagnosed in Haiti. If Haitian refugees had brought ASF virus infected pork into the U.S., it was estimated that it would have taken over $14 billion to eradicate it from the U.S. This was because of the lengthy incubation period. By the time that the virus would have been discovered, the disease would have spread throughout the United States.

Therefore, as a precautionary measure, the United States Department of Agriculture (USDA) spent $14 million to kill every single pig in Haiti. There is no treatment for most viral diseases. The only method of handling such a situation is to slaughter the infected animals. I was recruited by the USDA to go down to Haiti and help with the eradication campaign.

Just before I was to leave for Haiti, I walked into the faculty lounge to get a cup of coffee. As I walked in the lounge, Frank Hayes, the director of the Southeast Cooperative Wildlife Disease Study Unit said in his typical gruff voice, "Now, Stew, when you go down to Haiti next week, I want you to do whatever those little teenage boys holding the uzies tell you to do when you go through the road blocks."

Pouring out a cup of coffee, I immediately replied, "Frank, I'll do whatever they tell me to do, if whatever they say is reasonable."

John Williams, a large animal veterinarian blurted out, "Hell, Stew, if they are holding uzies, whatever they say, IS REASONABLE."

I must say that in Haiti, I met both some of the most vicious and most gentle people. My experience there could easily fill another book.

WHERE IS MECCA?

One of my colleagues was Mustafa Sali, an Egyptian veterinarian, who worked for the USDA in Okeechobee, Florida. We traveled together throughout Haiti at one period. We stayed in dormitory like places belonging to various government agencies. At one place, Mustafa and I shared a very small room that held only two small cots right next to each other.

One evening before dinner Mustafa said, "Do you mind if I say my prayers?"

"Not at all Mustafa; go right ahead. If you like, I can leave the room."

"No, no, that will not be necessary. You can stay right here. No problem."

We had recently arrived at this particular camp site and the sky was very cloudy. I was pretty sure which direction was north, because I have an interest in orientation wherever I go. However, because of the clouds apparently Mustafa was not sure. He first of all stood between the two beds facing north, bowed his head and mumbled some words. Then he took a bath towel, placed it on the floor between the beds, knelt down and bowed his head due north. Again he mumbled some words which I could not hear; that concluded his prayer.

Being sensitive to his religion and basically ignorant of Islamic dictates, I was hesitant to suggest that he may have not been facing Mecca during his prayers. Therefore, several days later, I said to Mustafa, "When you say your prayers, do you always have to face Mecca?"

"Of course, that is what we are supposed to do every time."

"What happens if you do not face Mecca?"

"Oh that is very bad."

"What happens if by accident, you are not facing Mecca when you say your prayers?"

His response still tickles me today. In a matter of fact tone, he said, "If you don't know, it don't matter."

IS MIAMI INSENSITIVE TO SPANISH SPEAKERS?

When I flew back to the U.S., as the plane taxied to the disembarkation gate at the Miami airport, the pilot made an important announcement. He said that we were going to a brand new international terminal. It was not yet open for business and had no services or personnel at this time. When we deplaned (that was his word) we were to follow the blue line on the brand new carpeting to a monorail which would then take us to the main terminal, where we were to go through customs.

So everybody did as the pilot instructed. As we entered the monorail, a voice over the loud speaker said in English, "Please prepare yourself for departure and secure yourself because this car leaves quite rapidly from the station." The train departed and about four people fell down immediately. It was then, only after the departure, that a second announcement came clearly over the loudspeaker saying, "Bienvenidios amigos, por favor, securidad ustedes, porque este - - - vehicle takes off quite rapidly from the station." [Partial translation, but you get the picture]. In other words, they warned the English speakers before the fact and the Spanish speakers after the fact. Is it any wonder that sometimes Spanish speakers feel like second class citizens?

MASAI MARA GAME PARK FIASCO

In December I presented a paper on veterinary geography at a virology conference in Nairobi, Kenya. I also wanted to investigate the possibility of laying the ground work for a grant application involving the collection of blood samples in order to test for Bovine Leukosis Virus (BLV) in both humans and cattle.

To that end, I had rented a car and drove to a very small village just west of Masai Mara game park. My wife and mother-in-law accompanied me. After contacting and setting up the connection with the local physician, we drove into the park from the west and went to the big resort in the center of the park. There we learned that to spend the night it would be extremely expensive.

When I said that we had decided not to spend the night and drive back to Nairobi, the clerk at the desk said that the eastern gate to the park closed at 5 pm and there was no way we could reach it since the time then was around 3:30 pm. When I looked at the map, I noticed that there was a junction headed west, from which we came that connected to a road the skirted the park on the north outside of the park. So, I asked if we could reach the western entrance to the park in time and take the other road. The clerk said yes that would be possible.

When I went to get gas, I saw that the cost was twice what I had paid at other gas stations along the way. I looked at my gas gauge and thought, I've got plenty of gas to reach a little town north of the park. I also felt reassured that the road on the map skirting the northern edge of the park was a big red line indicating that the road was a major highway and not a minor secondary road.

Therefore, without any trepidation, we took off for the junction to the western entrance of the park, which we reached around 4:30 pm. To my horror, as we embarked onto the road that had been demarked with a big red line and skirted the northern edge of the park, huge pot holes appeared. There were places where there was room for only one car to pass and there were no other cars, or activity of any kind. We had to ford streams, and as darkness arrived, I had to decide whether to take one road or the other as we came upon cross roads. Since there were no road signs or directions of any kind, I had to judge which road seemed to be used the most by estimating those roads that had less grass growing in the middle of the two trails of tire tracks.

The only signs I saw at intersections were oriented in the opposite direction. The only signs were for "Fig Tree Farm". I saw signs that stated at first, "Fig Tree Farm 35 miles." Then successively, there were signs saying that Fig Tree Farm was 55 miles, 75 miles and 90 miles. But never a sign about where we were going.

As it was pitch dark, with no moon light and we appeared hopelessly lost, I heard my mother-in-law say from the back seat, "Stewart, you've taken the wrong road." Lin, responded, "Now is no time to panic."

I tried to reassure them both that I knew what I was doing and thank god it was dark and they did not see my white knuckles clutching the steering wheel of the car. Because the road was so bad, I hardly ever felt that it was safe to go faster than 20 or 30 miles per hour because I was frightened of hitting high center and tearing a hole in the oil pan and ruining the motor.

Another concern I had at the time, was that we might be headed into Tanzania accidentally, where the shiftas (bandits) had machine gunned some tourist vans that very morning at the southern border of the park. On top of this, I became worried about the gas remaining in the tank. Since we were driving so slow and only in first or second gear most of the time, it was taking forever to make progress across the terrible roads.

At one point we saw what looked like a train, with lights like in a row of windows, but suddenly each of the lights dispersed in different directions. The lights were the reflection from the eyes of zebras that were all standing in a straight line looking at us.

In another crisis, a bridge was out and the stream had very steep sides. I thought about getting out and trying to determine how deep the water was. Also, I was worried that either the front of the car or the rear of the car might get stuck in the bottom of the stream bed. But then I thought, gosh, there might be lions roaming around with an empty belly, who would relish the thought of a tasty foreign dessert. So, I just gunned the motor and roared across and luckily we bounded to the other side successfully without an incident.

Around 10 pm, we approached a guard house with a barrier across the road. I walked up to the guard house and there was a black African eating an apple. When I said excuse me, he jumped up and dropped his apple. He heeded my request to open the gate and we immediately pulled into a small town. There was a gas station on the left side of the road. The attendant was locking up one of the gas pumps. He had to turn on the electricity, but happily filled up our gas tank that was right on empty. Just a few minutes later, he would have closed and gone home for the night.

So, all is well that ends well. We were just plain lucky.

1981

FIRST FULBRIGHT SENIOR RESEARCH AWARD
I returned to India in the spring of 1981 to determine whether or not Bovine Leukosis Virus (BLV) existed in India in the state of West Bengal. This project entailed bleeding both native and crossbred cattle at various locations and performing an immunological test to see if they possessed antibodies to BLV. As I recall, about 10% of both categories of cattle demonstrated evidence of BLV.

Once again I had to hand carried several hundred Petri dishes with me. This time there was no problem going through customs. At the conclusion of my project I attended the Fulbright year-end conference in Darjeeling, a town in the foothills of the Himalayas in West Bengal. The conference was held at a 5 star hotel. All of the waiters wore white gloves and everything was squeaky clean.

I asked to have access to the kitchen to burn the Petri dishes that I had utilized for my investigations. When I went into the kitchen, I was absolutely appalled at the filth and black grime that prevailed everywhere. It was a shock. But at least they kept up the illusion of perfect hygiene outside of the kitchen.

1982

A NEW YEAR'S EVE PARTY TO REMEMBER
Mardy and Fred Shirley had a New Year's eve party at their house which most of the Unitarians in Athens attended. It was a great party. Fred and Mardy, Bill and Elizabeth Sutton and Lin and I hung around after everybody else had left. After we had solved most of the problems of the world and had exhausted sex, religion and politics as topics in our inebriated discussions, we together tackled the problems of the future, the cost of living and the yearn to travel the world.

In our drunken stupor, we all decided to sell every material thing that we collectively possessed and all chip in to buy a big yacht and sail the 7 seas of the world. So as we all said goodbye around 5:30 or 6:00 am to straggle home, we were all in agreement to do the deed and each of us vowed to sell everything by the next New Year's eve.

Luckily, when we sobered up the next day and thought about it in more detail, we all agreed that perhaps that might not be the best scenario to seriously consider in a hasty manner. As it turned out, within a year or so, Mardy and Fred and Bill and Elizabeth were all divorced. Had we all kept our word to do the deed and sailed around the world, disaster might have occurred. I can imagine a boat full of angry people at each other's throats and Lin and I knowing nothing about sailing a boat. That would turn out as a recipe for a great tragedy.

1983

PUBLISHED MY FIRST BOOK:
My book, *The Geographical Distribution of Animal Virus Diseases* was published by Academic Press. This was no great literary achievement. It was just a series of world maps depicting where the different viral diseases had been authentically diagnosed, with a capsulized summary of pertinent information and contacts. I wanted to dedicate the book to the taxpayers of the state of Georgia because they paid my salary while I was writing the book. However, my editor at Academic Press would absolutely not allow it. She said that things like that are just not done. I said, so what, it is the truth. But she obviously prevailed. I, therefore, dedicated the book to Lin, but I told my mother that she could have the movie rights. I accumulated the royalties I earned to do something special. Something special turned out later to be flying lessons.

1984

MY SON PHIL AND THE LOS ANGELES OLYMPICS
My son Phil was 22 years old and he came over from Australia to be with me in early 1984. I had bought tickets to attend the Los Angeles Olympics and we drove across the country. The only thing that my son really wanted to do in the United States was to go to the Jack Daniels distillery in Tennessee. He and his buddies would drink Jack Daniels,

get drunk and call the distillery on the phone from Australia. So, he really wanted to go there; which we did.

During our tour of the facilities in a group of about 40 people, our guide gathered us together so that each person was standing around a huge opened vat of fermenting whiskey. He said, "If you take your hand, you can reach over the edge and sort of wave it upward, then you can smell the carbon dioxide."

Simultaneously, without saying a word to each other, Phil and I both leaned over and pushed our whole face into the open vat and each took a big sniff. It was just like someone had jammed a knife into our nasal mucosa. We each winched and said, ouch. None of the other tourist had been that stupid. It was remarkable to me that Phil and I both did it spontaneously on the spur of the moment.

When I met Phil when he first arrived I told him that since he was an adult, I did not want to boss him around. However, I did have one rule and that was that I would not tolerate his taking any drugs of any kind. That if he did take any drugs, that would wreck our relationship and I would have nothing to do with him.

During the Olympics we saw Saudi Arabia play against Morocco in soccer at the Rose Bowl in Pasadena. After the match as we were walking back, we stopped to admire a pickup truck with huge oversized tires. We talked with the owner for a while and then started to walk back to our car. Suddenly, I noticed that Phil was not with us. I went back to the pickup truck and as I came around the fender, I saw Phil take a big drag from a marijuana cigarette.

I was furious. I just turned on my heels and started back toward our car without saying a word, but he knew that I had seen him smoking the evil weed. I felt all of my blood flow into my hands and they became hard as rocks. I had the inclination to turn around and start to beat him with my fists. Phil immediately knew that I was extremely angry and he started apologizing profusely. I just never said a word.

I told him later that I thought it might be a good idea if he would stay in California and not come back to Georgia. So, he stayed with my sister, Franni and got a job in Los Angeles.

145

Later on, he decided to go back to Australia as his half-brother was in need of his help. He called and said that he wanted to come back to see me. I told him that I would not pay for his plane ticket to do so and that he could just go on back. Unbeknownst to me at the time, my sister paid for his plane ticket and he did come back to Georgia and I am so glad that he did. We were able to reform our friendship and respect for each other and when he left to go back to Australia we both had a better feeling about each other.

I found out after Franni's premature death due to breast cancer, that she had paid for Phil's airline ticket to come back to see me.

LEARNING TO FLY

One afternoon when my lab tech and I were preparing a test for the veterinary students a plane flew over the veterinary school and we both watched it through the windows. I said, "Gosh, I have always wanted to learn how to fly."

My lab tech, Craig Player, said, "I have too. Someone told me that you can buy a book on how to fly for $12."

"Just a minute, Craig; I'm going to run out for a minute and I'll be right back."

I drove immediately to the airport and went to Sonny's Flight School. I talked with Sonny for about a half hour and agreed to take flying lessons starting the next week. He sold me a book on how to fly, but it was $34.

I told Sonny that I had heard that one of the most dangerous things about flying was the maintenance of the air craft. I said, "How do I know that you maintain your plane always in good shape?"

With a sly grin, he responded, "'cause, I'll be up there with ya."

When I came back into the lab, I showed Craig the book and told him that it was much more than $12, but that was a good thing; because I had already invested such a huge sum, I would be motivated to see the flight school through to the end.

The next day, when Craig came to work he told me that he had stopped by the airport on this way home and also bought the book. We started to learn to fly together and it was great having someone else to talk to about the training.

Once when I went up in the air with Sonny, I turned to him and said, "Have you ever not been able to teach someone how to fly?"

He said, "Not up until now."

1985

In 1985 I presented results of my scientific investigations in Morocco, Italy, England and Australia. Each conference was memorable for various reasons.

MOROCCO

This was a virology conference. I found out before the conference if there were any students at the University of Georgia (UGA) from Morocco. I met one and he gave me something to give to his brother when I went to the conference. His brother met me and offered to take me around to see the sights of Rabat, the capital of Morocco which was the venue of the conference.

As we drove around and he would park his car, he would always give a few coins to a man standing around to provide the security for his car. In every single case (four separate times) the man receiving the money was missing his right hand. After the third time, I said to him, "Isn't it ironic that you are giving money to a thief to watch your car?"

Rather indignant, he replied, "What do you mean? I am not giving any thief money."

"Well, I noticed that each of the men that you give money to watch your car has their right hand missing. I heard that Islamic law says that if a man steals something, that his right hand is cut off."

"Oh no, those people are not thieves. They lost their hands in the war."

"What war was that?"

"Oh, you know, the war."

"No, I don't know about THE war. Which war was it?"

"I don't know. It was just the war."

Our discussion ended there. It is inconceivable to me that all of these men lost their hand in any war and they all suffered the same exact injury.

Another episode was interesting. About five of the participants at the conference were selected to go meet with the minister of agriculture. We all went to his office and the entire conversation was in French. Toward the end I understood only two words from the entire meeting. The minister said, ". . . unique experie-once."

Wherever I go, I always try to learn just some of the basic words in the local language. Even if I can exchange a few pleasantries, the natives always appreciate it. In my desire to always save money, I had purchased an airline ticket that was for more than one week. Therefore, when the conference was over, most everyone else left to go home.

I had nothing to do, so I bought a round trip train ticket to Meknes, a city about 100 miles away. When I got off of the train, I just wandered around taking the bigger streets toward the city center. Suddenly, this very big imposing Moroccan man walked right up to me and grabbed my arm and said in halting English, "Come, we go Kazbah."

As he had grabbed my arm quite tightly, I could not easily extract it. I turned to him and said the only Arabic word I had remembered, "No, shucri", which means, "no thanks".

His eyes got big and a big smile came across his face and he said, "Oh, you know my language!" He released my arm and was very kind and after I explained I had very little money, he lost interest and left.

ROME

I gave a paper at the Society for International Development and Bernadette Allard also attended the conference. She was an assistant to the director of the UGA Office of International Development. I eventually took her job when she retired in 1995. At any rate, she and I and several other folks from Athens, GA were going to go to the opening session. We went to the subway station and you needed the correct change or a ticket to pass through the turnstile. I had the correct coins and passed through. Bernadette did not have the change and none of the others had any change either.

Bernadette, speaks French and English fluently and she had to go above ground to a kiosk to buy a subway ticket. However, something got lost in translation of Italian to French or English (she tried both languages). When she came back down, she was in a hurry, so she slipped the ticket into the slot and expected the turnstile to move forward and admit her. Unfortunately, the Kiosk clerk had misunderstood and issued her a ticket for the next day. The result of this error was that Bernadette did a complete flip over the stationary turnstile and landed flat on her back.

At least she had accomplished her goal of getting on the other side. So our group, concerned about the valuable time we had lost, ran down the stairs to where the trains come into the station. I remember, worrying about missing the opening session. So when we went through an opening onto the platform a train was waiting right there. Immediately, we jumped onto the train.

I anticipated that the train was going in a certain direction, so I grabbed onto a pole in the middle of the aisle with both hands. Then I braced myself for a rapid acceleration by leaning completely backwards. Unfortunately, the train did accelerate rapidly, but in the opposite direction from that which I had anticipated. The results of this was that I was spun around 180 degrees and in the process almost knocked down about three people standing around me.

MELBOURNE

I was standing on a street corner, not too far from the University of Melbourne, where the conference was to take place. I was looking at a small map to see exactly where I should go when I crossed the street. A

149

car on the other side of the road, as it passed through the intersection had an occupant who hollered out the window, "How 'bout dem dogs!"

The comment was directed at me by an unknown person. What was so remarkable is that, that statement is heard every Saturday throughout Georgia during football season. The bulldog is the mascot of the team and that is what everybody says whenever the team does well.

I racked my brain trying to figure out, how on earth the person in that car knew I was from Georgia. The only way they could have known was that he saw my bright red UGA tie. A few years earlier during a fund raiser the tie was offered for sale. It was bright red, with repeating icons of UGA in black.

NOTTINGHAM

The interesting aspect of this conference was the trip to downtown Nottingham. The city government had made a pedestrian only downtown out of about 8 square blocks. They simply covered all of the streets from about the second or third story with what looked like plexiglass. Thus, rain or shine the folks could walk on the adequately illuminated wide streets protected from the elements.

The person who gave his presentation immediately before mine was very interesting. He measured the blood levels of old folks at a nursing home for vitamin D. He did this in early spring when the old folks came out to sun themselves. The levels were correlated with the amount of sunshine they were exposed to, by measuring the x-ray film badge changes in density because of the absorption of UVB radiation.

There was one lady who had a much higher level of vitamin D than anyone else, but had the same amount of UVB exposure. When he examined the data in more detail, he noticed that she was the only one who wore short sleeved shirts.

DEATHS IN ROUTE FROM ROME TO LONDON

I left Rome by train and traveled to Geneva, Switzerland. There I conferred with veterinarians at the World Health Organization (WHO) about viral diseases and the ecology of cattle. When I walked in the main entrance, there was a display case of book jackets with a big sign that said in English, "Critique's Choice" and at first I couldn't believe my eyes, because there was the book jacket from my book on *The Geographical Distribution of Animal Virus Diseases.*

 I went into the library and talked with the administrator. I asked if there truly was a group of critiques who selected the book covers to put into the case, or was it just something to do with the book jackets. According to my suspicions, she acknowledged that there had not been any critiques involved at all. It was just something to do with the book covers.

When I talked with the chief veterinarian, he asked me where I was headed next. I told him I was going to Munich to see Dr. Bateman about computerizing my book. He said, "Haven't you heard?"

I said, "Heard what?"

"Dr. Bateman died last Friday. He died of a heart attack on a beach in Portugal."

I explained that I had no idea but that I would go there anyway and see people at his lab if they would be available.

Dr. Bateman, had originally asked me to come on a Monday, but later called me and said it would be better if I arrived on Tuesday. He said that he had arranged a seminar by a noted virologist to give an invited lecture on rabies on Monday. So I had changed my schedule to go to WHO on Monday.

When I arrived at the lab on Tuesday morning, I asked a member of Dr. Bateman's research team how the lecture went on rabies the day before. He responded to that question with, "Haven't you heard?"

I said, "Heard what?"

He replied, "Herr Doctor from Berlin died of a stroke over the week-end."

The next day I took the train to Paris where I went to the Organization of International Epizootics. There, I related my consternation at being told of Dr. Bateman and the invited lecturer's deaths. My contact then looked at me with some surprise and said, (I'll swear this is true), "Haven't you heard?"

I said, "Heard what?"

He said, "Dr. Bateman's widow committed suicide yesterday."

My next stop was London and at the veterinary facility I visited there, I didn't ask about anybody and never mentioned Dr. Bateman, for fear that there would be another death about which I had not yet heard.

1986

SECOND FULBRIGHT FELLOWSHIP TO INDIA

This study was to resurvey the villages that I had studied in 1967 and 1977 and to again measure the differences in the human and cattle populations. Once again significant differences were found. The cross breeding program was expanded and the number of working bullocks was reduced. Once again fascinating experiences occurred, but are too numerous to include here.

1987

NATIONAL GEOGRAPHIC GRANT

During my Fulbright investigation, I was awarded a National Geographic grant to study the difference in productivity between the native and crossbred cattle. Unexpectedly, I found that the crossbred cows were more efficient energetically, at least in the initial crossbred offspring.

NATIONAL ACADEMY OF SCIENCES GRANT

While I was in India I received word that my competitive grant application for similar studies of cattle in China was accepted. I flew back to Ann Arbor, Michigan from Calcutta for a 3 day meeting with the other grantees. One day I was in 90 degree sweltering heat and the next in almost freezing temperatures in Ann Arbor.

Always wanting to get oriented in new locations, I asked the cleaning lady which way was north. She answered, "I don't have a clue."

"Well, just tell me from which direction does the sun come up." I countered.

"I don't remember. I haven't seen the sun in months. I almost forgot what it looks like."

Every time I leave India and come back to the USA, I get sick with giardia which is an intestinal parasite. Once again, the second day in Ann Arbor, the nausea set in and I felt terrible. I went to a pharmacy and told the pharmacist my problem and then asked if I could write a prescription for my dog for a giardiacide. I explained I was licensed to practice in the state of California, but not Michigan. He said, "You can write it and I can dispense it. What you do after that, is entirely up to you." So I wrote out the script and handed it to him. He started laughing and I asked him why. He said that my dog's name was amusing. For my fictitious dog's name, I had written, "Wolf".

ON TO CHINA

I went to Beijing in September. I had been in Calcutta the month before. The contrast was unbelievable. In Calcutta, the traffic was always in a jam or so chaotic that you literally had to fear for your life. There were kamikaze taxi drivers, maneuvering around bullock carts, dare devil motorcyclist, tongas (carts pulled by men) with heavy loads, trucks, busses , streetcars, beggars, etc. It was said that the taxi driver could not go anywhere without honking the horn. So everybody else did it as well. The noise was deafening.

In Beijing, it was surrealistic. There were signs everywhere with a picture of a horn in a circle with a red diagonal line drawn through it, meaning do not honk your horn. There were thousands of bicycles everywhere. There was no noise. All of the traffic lights worked. Everyone stopped and went in an orderly way in an eerie silence. Almost everyone was wearing a Mao suit, either of dark blue or olive drab color.

Like in India, I could fill a book with what I observed and the experiences that I lived through in China. Just before I left to go to

China, I asked John Williams, a veterinary colleague who had just returned from his first trip to China, what was the best piece of advice he could give me about going to China. He answered, "Take a fork".

1988

CONCEPTION OF MY SECOND SON, COLIN

When Lin and I got married in 1977 I told her that I didn't care whether or not we had any children because I was a proven sire and had a 15 year old son living in Australia with his mother. I added, if you want children that's fine with me. If you do not want children, that's fine with me also.

During our stay in the study village in Shandong Province in China and Lin had reached the age of 39, I thought that if she wanted a kid, we had better get busy out of fear of Down's syndrome. So, one afternoon I took the microscope outside, went upstairs after lunch, masturbated and collected the ejaculate onto a glass slide. I put a cover slip on the slide and showed Lin thousands of my healthy sperm.

As she peered into the microscope I said, "What you are looking at are thousands of little Odend'hals wanting to meet your eggs. If you think you might want to have a baby, we should not wait any longer."

She said that she thought that I did not want to have kids, so she had resigned herself to that strategy. So, she said yes; maybe we could try to have a baby. Sure enough within a week or so, conception occurred in China. Months later when she found out that she was pregnant she would say, "When I found out that I was pregnant, I felt like a teenager because we only did it once without protection and I got pregnant."

1989

NEAR DEATH EXPERIENCE

As Lin was pregnant with a due date in March, she stayed home and I went to China alone for the month of January. In my study village, it was 42 degrees Fahrenheit in the little room where I ate my food, 32 degrees where I slept and 22 degrees outside where I went to the outhouse. Needless to say, I didn't hang around in the toilet reading the newspaper. The only heat was from a small pot of coal that released more dust than heat. I got a cold and a severe respiratory infection.

The cold was complicated by asthma and I could breathe only with great difficulty. One night, sitting up in my bed during the sleepless night, I honestly could not tell whether or not my inspirations were actually delivering air into my air sacs. My thoracic muscles were tired from the forced breathing in and out, that for a split second, I thought, "This is it. I cannot oxygenate or to continue trying to breathe. It is just too much trouble. I will just let myself die to get away from all of this trouble."

In another split second I remembered the sonogram that Lin had sent to me the day before of the fetus's developing bones of his little hand. This hit me distinctly and I decided to continue the struggle to survive. I woke up Andrew Kipnis, another American researcher and told him that I needed to go the hospital. After some discussion with the village elders, that is what I did. That is another remarkable story that there is not room for, in this type of communication.

As an aside, I used to take the sonogram around with me and tell some of the villagers that it was a picture of my son, which seemed to perplex them greatly.

BIRTH OF COLIN CLARK ODEND'HAL

Lin had trouble with hypertension and other complications, so our son was delivered by Caesarian section a month early. I was privileged to be in the operating room at the time of delivery.

Lin was separated from the surgeons by a raised piece of cloth. I was standing at the border of the cloth so I could see both Lin and the surgeons. Lin was completely awake and a nurse or midwife was seated right next to her and talking to her the entire time. Even though Lin had received a spinal anesthetic, she could feel the tugging and manipulation of the body wall, as the surgeons struggled to remove the baby.

All during the process, I could see Lin was extremely anxious and had a furrowed brow and winched periodically. In other words she was under a great deal of stress and her facial expressions demonstrated that in no uncertain terms.

However, once the baby was removed from the womb, cleaned up and taken over to her to see for the very first time, one of the most remarkable transitions occurred I have ever witnessed. Once she laid eyes on him, all of the signs of stress in her face disappeared and she had the most angelic relaxed expression on her face and she said, "Why he's beautiful." Not just "beautiful", but "BEAU-TI-FUL".

The other factor that impressed me so much was the following. Once the baby was removed from the uterus, He was covered in slimy slippery white cheesy looking material. Undoubtedly, this natural material acts to facilitate the movement through the birth canal. But I had never been aware of it before.

AFTERMATH OF TIANANMEN SQUARE

In September I went back to China. I had been advised by high ranking officials connected with the state department that it would be safe to do so. When I arrived in Beijing, there were tanks and soldiers on all of the bridges. In my study village, every night on the evening TV news there were stories lauding the heroic roles of the soldiers and the military in stopping the revolutionary democratic thugs. There were shots of soldiers recuperating in hospitals. The distorted propaganda turned my stomach.

The village elders were constantly talking to me trying to justify the massacre. Finally, I just could not stand it anymore. I told my interpreter, if they mentioned Tiananmen Square one more time I was going to walk out of the room. He hesitated, and I told him, you tell them that and they can tell by my manner that I mean it. After he allegedly told them, they did not raise the issue again.

When I left by train by myself, I am sure, in retrospect, there was a spy in my compartment. One of my bunk mates in the overnight trip back to Beijing was a graduate from Kansas State University who spoke prefect English. He was very pleasant and I enjoyed talking with him until we went to sleep.

In the morning as we were about an hour from arriving at Beijing, he became very nervous and suddenly said, "What do you think about the situation that happened in Tiananmen Square?"

I responded, "I thought it was a tragedy for all concerned."

He countered, "The VOA lied, you know."

"What's the VOA? I don't know what that is."

"The voice of America."

"How did they lie?"

"They said that thousands died and it was really only about a hundred."

"Were you there? Did you see it?"

"No, no, I was not there," he stammered.

"Did you see it on TV?" I asked.

"No, I did not see it on TV."

"Then how do you know what to believe. I saw it on TV. There is no doubt in my mind that unarmed peaceful people were killed."

He stopped talking and I said nothing until we got to Beijing where we exchanged reserved goodbyes.

TOILET TRAINING OR LACK THEREOF

I guess Colin must have been close to 9 months old and we were having trouble getting rid of diapers. Colin just couldn't seem to get the message to tell us when he wanted to defecate.

One day, I came home and when I walked in the door, I saw that Colin just had on a T-shirt and no diapers at all. I walked into the kitchen and said to Lin, "Why isn't Colin wearing any diapers?"

157

She responded, "Well, we are having so much trouble potty training him that I thought I would try something different."

"Isn't that a little dangerous? He could defecate anywhere and we might not know about it."

"Well, let's see. Give it a chance."

Immediately after this exchange, I walked back into the living room and there on the hard wood floor was one of the biggest turds I have ever seen. I was amazed that Colin had obviously produced it.

"Lin," I cried, "come look at this."

She walked into the living room, looked down at this oversized turd and hollered at Colin, "Did you do this?"

Actually, I was quite offended, because if he had not done it, the only other suspect around was me and how could she even think that I could do such a thing.

Colin looked up at his mother, eye ball to eye ball and stated very clearly, "I did not."

I said to Lin, "Don't look at me; I did not do it either and obviously Colin is lying."

MY MOTHER MOVES TO ATHENS, GEORGIA

During one of my mother's visit to see us, Lin remarked, "Why don't you think about moving back here to Athens?"

My mother said, "That's not a bad idea."

After living in Southern California for over 35 years, I was really surprised that she did move to Athens. The attraction was, of course, that cute little rascal Colin. My mother had recently sold her travel agency and it was great to have her nearby.

1990

FLIGHT DELAYS: SAN FRANCISCO, USA AND TOKYO, JAPAN

I had five trips to China. Two of those journeys were interrupted by overnight flight delays; one in San Francisco and one in Tokyo. The contrast of the organization or lack thereof was amazing to me.

The first delay occurred in Tokyo. Within a very short period of time, over one hundred passengers were herded down some stairs to several waiting busses that took us to a very large hotel only a few miles away. When we walked into the hotel, there was a special area with a very long slightly curved table with about 15 or 20 clerks standing behind the table. The delayed passengers filled up a line in front of each clerk in numbers of 5 or 6 and immediately received the key to their room, and a chit for a meal ticket worth about $7.

The second flight delay occurred in San Francisco. We were sitting for at least an hour in a United Airline 747 waiting for some unseen and unmentioned delay. Finally, the pilot said, "Please accept our sincere apology. There is a mechanical problem that necessitates us to abort this flight. Please go to the United service counter after leaving the plane."

When we got to the service counter, there was no information available. After this large group of people had been standing around waiting for some information, a representative appeared and said in a loud voice, "There are no more flights to Tokyo today. We will put you all up in a hotel for tonight. There is a bus in the parking lot that will take you to your hotel." Then the representative disappeared.

The parking lot was huge. There were no signs or directions, other than, "There is a bus in the parking lot." I looked around and saw a single bus away off toward the back of the huge parking lot. It was a very long walk. I was the first one there and I asked the bus driver if this bus was to take the passengers to the hotel. He indicated that it was. I asked where were the other buses to take the rest of the people to the hotel. He said that they only had one bus. I asked how far away was the hotel, and he responded that it was about 40 miles away. I said, "You mean that the other people will have to wait until you go back and forth to take the remainder of the people to the hotel?" He said, that was the way it was.

So, our flight was supposed to have left San Francisco around 12 noon. I got to the hotel along with the other 40 or 50 who were on the first bus around 4 pm. When we walked into the hotel (I was second in line), there was only one clerk behind a very narrow check-in desk. I got my key, went up to my room and called a friend in Palo Alto to meet me for dinner at the hotel.

I looked out the window periodically and saw another bus unload around 5:30 pm. Because I had not heard back from my friend, I decided to lay down and went to sleep accidentally. Around 8 pm the phone rang and my friend said that she would be coming over. When she got there about 9 pm, they were still unloading a bus from the airport. Unbelievable.

1991

COMMUNIST EMPLOYMENT IN CHINA

During one of my trips to Beijing I witnessed the invasion of Mongolia. A dust storm from the north had totally reduced the visibility to only about one city block. What amazed me was the city had employed women to sweep the streets. These women were working with their brooms sweeping the streets in an obvious exercise of futility. They all had what looked like nylon stockings wrapped around their faces presumably to limit the inhalation of the dust. It apparently didn't matter why they were sweeping. It was just their job and they had to do it, whether it made any difference of not.

1992

"A STRANGE MAN IN THE HOUSE"

Originally, there were 8 of us that received grants from the National Academy of Sciences for the China studies. Later on, three more researchers joined our program. Each year we would all meet at a conference to compare and share data. One year we all met in Los Angeles.

Bill Chang, had moved from Michigan to Washington, D.C. and taken a new job with the National Science Foundation. He came down to eat dinner about 8 pm and when he sat down next to us, he said, "I just had the shock of my life."

160

I said, "What happened?"

"I called back to my house in Bethesda where the local time was around 11 pm and a strange man answered my phone. I was so shocked, I hollered who is this? And the answer came back in a broken voice, 'This is Chris'. That's my 14 year old son. His voice is changing which I never heard before and I thought it was a strange man."

When I told this story to Fred Smith, my partner in the histology course that we taught at UGA together, he said, "Your friend Bill was right the first time. If he had a teenager in his house, he did indeed have a strange man in his house."

1993

THE CHURCH'S HANDICAP RAMP

Ray McNair's 95 year old father moved about in a very heavy motorized wheelchair. Every Sunday, it took four to six of us to lift him up the six steps to enter the Unitarian-Universalist Fellowship Hall. This procedure continued for months. One day, like a miracle there was a ramp which allowed Mr. McNair to motor up the front steps by himself. The minister just stated that the ramp had been donated by an anonymous patron. Years later, I found out that the anonymous donor had been my mother. She never told me and I wonder what other good works she did that no one knows about.

1994

"IT FELL FROM THE SKY"

Our Unitarian-Universalist Fellowship in Athens had a pot luck supper every Wednesday evening. It usually started around 6:30 pm when we had wine and snacks and then ate the pot luck meal between 7 and 8 pm. I was in charge of buying the wine and usually showed up early to set up the bar.

One Wednesday, as I opened up the fellowship a new member and her daughter came in. Her daughter and Colin went outside to play in the playground, which was fenced-in while I got the wine ready. The new member said to me, "Do you think it would be a good idea if we went outside to watch the children?"

"Sure, that's a good idea."

As I opened the door to the playground, Colin came running up toward me pointing to his throat as he approached. Immediately, I saw that he couldn't breathe. Instinctively, I just picked him up, turned him upside down and shook him violently toward the ground and jerked him back up again. A round big blue ball gum fell out of his mouth.

I said rather sternly, "Where did you get that?"

"It fell from the sky." was his response.

I had to laugh. I was so grateful that the new member had suggested that we go outside to watch the kids, because who knows what might have happened otherwise.

COLIN'S QUESTION BRINGS APPLAUSE

One Christmas, Lin, Colin and I went to Fort Davis State Park in West Texas. That was the year for some reason, the government closed all of the national parks for several weeks because of political budget disagreements. We went to tour the University of Texas McDonald Observatory, along with a large contingent of people who had been turned away from Big Bend National Park, because of the park closures.

The tour began in front of one of the older telescope buildings and consisted of the tour guide taking all of us (about 50 people) to the edge of the mountain. There in very cold windy weather, the tour guide went on and on about the laser complex that could be seen in the valley. He said that the laser beam is bounced off of the moon and that any small changes in distances could be detected. He told us more than most of us really wanted to know about this aspect and people were cold and visibly uncomfortable.

Colin and I were standing close to the tour guide. He finally had finished his presentation and everyone hoped that we would now go into the telescope building and get warm. Unfortunately to most

162

people, the guide, instead of leading us away from the edge of the mountain, said, "Are there any questions?" With a few audible groans in the back of the pack of freezing tourists, Colin raised his hand. At 6 years old, I thought to myself, 'What kind of question does he have, since most of the presentation had been sort of technical?' Colin then said, very clearly, "When are we going to go inside?" There was a spontaneous outburst of applause. Needless to say, I was proud of my boy and pleased that he said, what everyone else was too polite to say.

NEIGHBORLY ADVICE

My neighbors, John and Johnna Miller had three boys; 1, 4 and 6 years of age. They loved to watch a kid's TV program called 'Wishbone'. This was about a very cute Jack Russell Terrier dog, who would day dream about being some historical hero, like Robin Hood, Zorro, or Davy Crocket. In the dreams, the dog would wear the appropriate attire of the hero and fight all of the other dressed up dogs. It was an entertaining way for the kids to learn of the hero's historical exploits.

Well, all of their sons constantly badgered them to buy them a Jack Russell terrier. So they finally caved in and bought a Jack Russell terrier for $350. John said that he wanted to have a fenced-in back yard. Johnna insisted that the cyclone fencing that John picked out, be the expensive kind with green coated wire so that it would blend in with the green forest behind their back yard. That was another $3,000.

When they had the fence built, then they bought the dog. When they put the dog in the back yard, the dog jumped over the fence within 30 minutes. So, John went and bought the material to fix a wire along the top of the fence and electrified the wire. The dog attempted to jump over the fence, but stopped because of the shock.

Within a day or two when they put the dog in the back yard, the dog dug under the fence. When I visited their house one time I looked out into their back yard and I could see where John had plugged up the holes under the fence at several spots with concrete bricks, boards, and assortments of rocks and boulders of various sizes. The appearance of the back yard was, to put it in one single word, atrocious.

Next, John turned to what he considered at the time a fool proof scheme. He built a dog run in the back yard. It was a 12 X 8 feet enclosure. It had chicken wire embedded in the ground; big heavy steel poles at the corners with chicken wire over the top of the cyclone fencing. He showed it to me when it was finished and it looked like it could hold a tiger. But, at least, he had cleaned up the ugly holes and taken down the ratty looking electrified wire from the top of the perimeter fencing. He explained triumphantly that he had finally "nipped the little bugger in the ass".

A couple of weeks later, when I asked him how things were going, he lamented the following story. He said that the dog unbelievably had chewed through the cyclone fence in the run. So, he ended up keeping the dog inside all of the time. He started walking the dog, which he didn't enjoy, but did not trust the kids to do it. Since the dog was inside all of the time, he began to bark all of the time. So he bought a "barkless collar" for the dog. Every time the dog would bark this collar sent an electrical shock that caused the dog to winch, yelp in pain and stop barking.

Unfortunately, shortly after he had purchased the collar, the family was watching TV (probably the "Wishbone" program) and John took the remote control for the TV and began changing channels. Every time he changed a channel, he noticed that the dog would jump slightly and yelp. Somehow the frequency of the channel changer turned on the electrified collar of the "barkless collar". To begin with John thought to himself 'What in the hell is wrong with the crazy dog?' By the time the cause of the dog's discomfort dawned upon him, one of the kids opened the door to the outside and the dog shot out the door.

They never saw the dog again after that. John said that he was not sorry to see the dog go. He figured that the dog had cost him close to $4,000 and was never fun as far as he was concerned. He said to me with pleading eyes, "Stew, if you ever get a dog for Colin, make sure it is one of the dumbest dogs in the world."

1995

OFFICE OF INTERNATIONAL DEVELOPMENT
I was visiting with my mother when I got a telephone call from the director of the Office of International Development at UGA. He asked

me to join his office half time. My current appointment was for 50% teaching and 50% research. I could pick whether I wanted to retain the teaching or the research appointment. I retained the teaching. My title would be assistant to the director instead of "assistant director", but it would amounted to the same thing. My job would be to acquire research and study grants for foreign national to come to UGA for training and graduate studies.

EUROPEAN CENTER OF ATLANTA (ECA)

Shortly after I joined the Office of International Development, the Vice-President for Services at UGA asked me to become the director of the European Center of Atlanta. This position was affiliated with the East-West Institute in New York City. With their help, the center stimulated cooperation and exchanges with the former communist countries of Central and Eastern Europe. The Board of Directors were prominent leaders in Atlanta. I agreed to become the director, even though I had a pretty full plate of activity. I taught the histology course to the veterinary students; I was president of the Athens Kiwanis club and chairman of the Georgia unit of Recording for the Blind, as well as active in the Unitarian-Universalist Fellowship, in addition to my new duties with the Office of International Development. But, I must say, there was never a dull moment and I enjoyed the rapid pace.

Matt Richardson, who was the second in command of the ECA, told me that I should email a really nice person in Slovakia, Marta Prosbova, who was also a veterinarian. I sent her an email and her response truly amazed me. Reading between the lines, I just knew that I would like her a lot. Little did I realize at that time that she would eventually end up my constant companion and the love of my life.

In November I traveled to Kosice (the second largest city in Slovakia) to meet with her and other university officials to set up an exchange program. She was away at the time, so I went to Budapest and came back. In Budapest, I was in a book store looking at a map of the region and saw on the map, that Kosice, was represented as Kashau. I thought to myself, "Ah, ah, when I go to the train station I will know to ask for a ticket to Kashau instead of Kosice."

When I went to the train station ticket counter, I got my ticket to Kosice. Watching the departure and arrival board, I looked for

Kashau, but never saw that name. On the board, there was the word Kassa, which left the time that I was supposed to leave for Kosice. Finally, I learned at the last minute from the information desk that Kassa was the Hungarian name for Kosice. The map that I saw in the book store was in German and the German word for Kosice was Kashau.

COLIN QUESTIONS NOAH

One evening as Colin and I were flipping through the channels on TV, we suddenly saw a picture of animals walking up a plank into a very big boat. It was a movie about Noah and the ark. I thought to myself, 'Well, this is educational for Colin, since he should have knowledge about our Judeo-Christian background.' So, I stopped changing channels and we both watched the program.

As the narrator was explaining that Noah was ordered by God to collect two of each species of animals on earth to save them from the flood that allegedly was supposed to destroy all living things on earth, Colin turned to me. Taking a piece of gum out of his mouth, he said to me, "Didn't that cause a lot of inbreeding?"

1996

BUILDING BRIDGES EXCHANGE PROGRAM

Just before the summer Olympics in Atlanta, a group of 35 educators from central and Eastern Europe came to Georgia. Since Marta was a veterinarian, she came to Athens and was my guest for several days. The group reassembled in a conference in Atlanta, the day before they traveled back to Europe. I fell irreversibly and madly in love with Marta.

In September, everyone who had hosted one of the members of the group in Georgia traveled to central and Eastern Europe to visit with their visitor's universities. Marta and I traveled to the veterinary schools in Budapest, Vienna and Brno in the Czech Republic. From that point on, we were in constant communication.

1997

MY MOTHER DIED

In 1992 we had moved into Athens city proper to be closer to my mother and closer to Colin's school. Also, I told my mother that although she was in complete control of her faculties, there may come a day when she might start to shuffle and I wanted a house that she could live in without any stairs. She laughed at the time about that and told all of her friends. Before I describe her demise, I should briefly tell about her time in Athens, as there were many memorable events.

She first moved from California to Athens in 1989. The first place she moved to, was a complex which consisted of part assisted living and part nursing home. She lived on the second floor with a small balcony that over looked a swamp. In the winter time there was a vulture roost and you could see hundreds of vultures flying in the sky at different times of the day. My mother was 75 years old, but in very good shape and she eventually concluded that she really didn't belong in such a facility. So she moved to a more appropriate apartment complex in Athens. It had a swimming pool and Colin enjoyed it.

One day visiting her I noticed that she complained of pain in her arm. I looked and saw that she had a cracked finger nail and I could see a red line traveling up from her nail along the inside of her arm. This appeared to me to be a lymphangitis with a possibility of serious consequences, so I took her immediately to the emergency room. There, they prescribed antibiotics after giving her an intra-venous injection of antibiotics.

The doctor said, that if she had not come in and received the injection, that a full blown septicemia could have developed. That could have proved fatal if the antibiotics happened to be delivered too late. Death would have resulted from the overwhelming proliferation of the bacteria in her blood.

When I came to see her the next day, she said that her whole arm became bright red and she watched it gradually go up her arm. She said further, that if the red line had reached a mole on her upper arm, she was going to call me in the middle of the night. However, the red line and heat stopped below the mole and the red line gradually regressed back down her arm and finally disappeared about dawn.

167

Our new house was about half a mile from my mother's apartment. Every Sunday morning I would walk through the forest that separated our residences and visited with her. The forest was part of the Athens YMCA Summer Camp Grounds. I used to tell people that I had a 75 acre back yard with four and one half miles of hiking trails. I never told anyone that I owned it, but it was like I owned it because I hardly ever saw anyone else on the trails that I used.

One time at my mother's house, I said to her, "Why are you so blue? You don't seem happy at all. Is something bothering you?"

She replied, "Louama died yesterday in Oklahoma City." Louama was one of my mother's best friends from high school.

I said, "Gosh Ma, I am so sorry. If you want, I will be willing to drive you to the Atlanta airport any time you want to go."

She said, "As a friend of mine told me once. One thing is for sure; why should I go to her funeral, because she certainly is not going to go to mine."

For my mother's 80th birthday in 1994, I took her along with Lin and Colin to the Chateau Elan resort for lunch and gave her 80 Hersey hugs (white chocolate) and 80 Hersey kisses (black chocolate) among other things. I told her then that since she was gone on various trips most of the time, she was paying half of her rent for nothing. Therefore, why didn't she move into our house to the downstairs bedroom with the private bath.

She agreed, but in her inimitable style, she eventually renovated our bonus room above the garage with the private back staircase. She also took the upstairs laundry room and had that made into a bathroom. Ironically, I had purchased the house so she could live on one floor in her old age, and she decided to live upstairs and added another bathroom, when we already had three bathrooms.

Shortly before she moved, I was talking to her on the phone early one morning from work. She had not been feeling good and I was concerned about her. She sounded confused and suddenly said, "I don't know which end of the phone I am speaking through."

I said, "I am coming right over there right now and taking you to the emergency room."

She said, "Please don't do that until you have talked with my doctor. I don't want to be admitted to the hospital on the strength of my veterinarian."

I replied, "I'll do that right now and I'll be over there immediately".

I called her doctor and the receptionist said he was with a patient. I told her that I was taking my mother to the hospital and he could meet us over there whenever he could.

The doctor and I had a difference of opinion over his treatment to begin with. He had prescribed estrogen replacement for her. When she told me that she was menstruating, I called and told him that it was ridiculous to give estrogen to an 80 year old lady and cause her to menstruate. He said that he would reduce the dose, but that it was important to prevent osteoporosis. What I did not know at the time was he was also giving her massive doses of calcium.

My mother was very confused and was admitted to the hospital. Tests showed that she had extremely high levels of calcium in her blood and that accounted for her symptoms and that all she needed to do was to "dry out" (allow the calcium to drop down to a normal level).

The next afternoon, as I was talking with her in her hospital room, suddenly my mother's eyes sort of fluttered and she said, "Gosh, I don't know what's coming over with me. I just felt so strange."

One minute later, a nurse came bounding into the room and said to my mother, "Are you all right?" To which she responded in the affirmative.

I asked, "Why are you so concerned?"

The nurse reacting less anxious stated, "I was looking at her heart monitor and suddenly it went flat, indicating that there were no heart beat."

The cardiologist came in a short time later. With his stethoscope on mother's chest, he said, "You are having arrhythmias right now. That is, your heart is skipping beats and is not beating regularly. We can fix that up with a pace-maker which I can put in this afternoon."

My mother moved into our upstairs renovated bonus room for only a short period of time and then she went back to Oklahoma City to attend her 62nd high school reunion. There, she danced the night away with Ray Anthony, the older brother of one of her high school heart throbs. Essentially, they fell in love. He was 83 and she was 81. Within a week of her return to Athens, she said that she was moving back to Oklahoma City. She and Ray Anthony then traveled every month to some part of the world. I had never seen her happier. Ray's kids told me the same thing about their dad.

While I was happy for my mother, I was sad to see her go. Colin, no doubt missed her a lot also. I wrote Ray, that my mother had always been a live wire, but he had put a spark in her I had never noticed before. He was very well off financially and I knew that he was not after her money and she was not after his money. They were just very happy together.

They had been in Spain and returned to Oklahoma City. Two days after the trip, my mother dropped a bottle of coca cola. She thought to herself how could I have done such a thing and then suddenly collapsed. She had a massive stroke. It paralyzed her right side of her body and she lost her ability to speak. I flew immediately to Oklahoma City. After several days in the hospital, she was moved to a nursing home.

The government program paid for the first three months of her stay, after that she had to come up with the cash somehow to stay in the nursing home. Again, I flew back to Oklahoma City and met with the trust officer at the bank to see how we were going to pay for the nursing home. Ray Anthony was there at that meeting. He had been with her every single day since her stroke.

Mother had given me legal power of attorney many years before. At the lunch table, the trust officer explained that with my mother's

170

dividends and investments, she could afford payments of $2,000 per month for the nursing home for a double room. However, it was Mr. Anthony's wish that she be in a private room and that was $3,000 per month. Further, Mr. Anthony had committed to pay $1,000 per month so that she could afford to stay in the private room.

As tears welled up in my eyes and I became completely speechless, the trust officer continued, with Ray Anthony sitting next to me, "I should add, that for Mr. Anthony to do this; it is really not a problem."

My mother was never able to communicate verbally. She did indicate displeasure and happiness at times, but it was so disconcerting not to be able to talk with her. She still showed her kindness and concern for others less fortunate than herself in the dining hall and wanted to help others somehow. Colin showed her how to fly a kite at one visit, which I know she enjoyed.

She passed away on September 18, 1997. Ray had a memorial service for her a day or so later. I did not attend the memorial service because I had a scheduled meeting in London with a group of Europeans. The meeting which I had organized, involved starting a cooperative veterinary library on an internet site. Before I left Oklahoma City, I explained that it was my mother's wish, not to have a memorial service per se, but to have a party to celebrate her life with alcohol and fun. She even had stipulated to me (and in writing) that money should be set aside for her friends from California to come to the party.

So, when I got back from Europe, Ray Anthony had a party at his house and it was packed with all of her friends and relatives and my brothers came also. No one from California came. All of her friends that I called were either too old to travel or had died.

MY SISTER, FRANNI, DIED
I have one full blood brother, two half-brothers and 5 half-sisters. Of all of them, Franni, was my favorite. My stepmother told me one time that my dad said that out of all of his kids, it was only me and Franni that never gave him any trouble or cause for concern. Franni developed breast cancer when she was around 47 years old. She went through chemotherapy and made a heroic stand against the disease for over three years. But eventually, she died in November of 1997.

The last time I saw her, I helped her pick out a trailer and then helped her move from her house in Woodland Hill, California to Calabassas, California. We were driving around doing errands and she stopped to call one of the other breast cancer patients in her support group. She came back to the car visibly shaken. I asked her what was the matter. She said that she called the person to tell her that one of the members of their support group had died. The lady's 12 year old son answered the phone and when she asked to speak to his mother, he said that she had died the week before. Franni, was totally discouraged at this news. My son Phil and her son, Evan scattered her ashes in the Santa Monica mountains west of Los Angeles. She was a wonderful lady.

1998

RETIREMENT AND ON TO ALBUQUERQUE, NEW MEXICO

In April, I decide to retire. Colin, as usual, was not doing very well in math in school and he was attending a public school where he was a minority and picked on, even by the girls. One big girl in his 5th grade class tried to bully him all of the time. So, I went on the internet and looked for a summer school out west that had a math course. After searching schools in Phoenix, Tucson, Colorado Springs and Albuquerque, I selected Albuquerque. Albuquerque Academy's web site had a real neat aerial photograph that I liked a lot.

In June, Colin and I went to ABQ in our RV. We camped out at the house of one of the teachers and house sat while they were on vacation. We fed and looked after their huge dog, 12 chickens and 15 piranhas. Yep, piranhas; we had to feed them thawed meat every day. Colin took math and a "how to study" course.

Colin would go to swim from 6 to 7 am and then had classes from 8 to 12. After I dropped him off, I would go to learn how to fly the powered parachute. In the evening, both Colin and I would go to learn how to fly. We had fun. Lin came out at the end of the 6 weeks summer school and we just were looking around and suddenly we bought this house.

Back in Athens we could not sell our house very easily and ended up staying one more year there. We did go back out to ABQ for the balloon fiesta and invited my high school buddies, Bernie Hodge and

Charles Schweinle along with their wives. Also my brother and his wife came down from Colorado. I also invited all of my new neighbors to a party. It was a good time.

This year is a blur. I went to Mexico with the Global Volunteers to teach English, traveled around and met Marta from time to time both in Europe and the US.

2000

THE WRONG ELDER HOSTEL

I signed up on the internet to attend an elder hostel in Phoenix, Arizona having to do with wildlife and nature photography. I drove out to Phoenix in my RV and pulled a motorcycle trailer. I had fun along the way. The morning of the first day after registration we were all (approximately 50 people) sitting down and the host started by saying "Welcome to the Tony Hillerman workshop and mystery lovers. . . ". What he said after that I do not remember. I looked to my right and to my left and folks on either side of me looked just as perplexed as I was.

After the first break, about five other people besides myself approached the host and explained that we had all signed up to attend a photographic workshop and not a Tony Hillerman discussion club. As it turned out, on the internet, as one scrolled down the page, the listing of the meeting place and time at the bottom pertained to the next workshop and not to the one described above. What's more, there were no obvious dividing line to separate the different workshops, so total confusion was the result.

2001

WORLD TRADE CENTER DISASTER

Colin was going to Menaul School near downtown ABQ and it was my day to take the car pool kids to school. As I was driving back home on the freeway, I heard about a plane hitting the world trade center. As I got home and turned on the TV, I saw the second plane hit the other tower building. The rest is history. In the days that followed with the revelation that Islamic militants were responsible, I tried to call the local mosque to tell them that I didn't believe that they in general were all militants and to give them some reassurance that there were Americans that did not hate all of them. They never answered the phone.

DOUBLE BYPASS OPERATION

In Athens before we moved, I used to exercise with these 5 pound dumb bells and do 100 repetitions of bicep curls. In ABQ, I was only able to do 50. One day, I thought I have to increase this to at least 55. When I did this, all of a sudden I experienced difficulty in breathing. It wasn't severe, but was noticeable and I thought, maybe I have asthma, but there was no wheezing. Out of curiosity, I took my pulse. To my surprise, I was having distinct arrhythmias, with significant periods of no pulse at all. Having had a college education, I whispered to myself, "Perhaps I should seek some professional advice here."

So I drove to my GP's office and told the receptionist that I thought I was having a heart attack. They whisk me in and put me on the electrocardiograph machine. The doctor took my pulse and said, everything looks completely normal. However, it would probably be prudent to send me to a cardiologist and I should go there immediately; which I did. The cardiologist said, that the history was not specific to anything, but it would be best to do a cardiolite test, where they could determine the flow of blood to the heart muscle; which they did the next day. The results suggested that there was impaired blood flow to one area of the heart muscle and I needed to have an angiogram. This demonstrated even to my untrained eye a 95% blockage to one of the major arteries in my heart.

The doctors wanted to put in a stent, which looks just like a coiled spring. It is inserted collapsed into the affected artery and is then expanded to keep it open. They said further that since my collateral circulation was good, it might be best, if I could wait a few weeks because there would be released on the market a new improved stent called a coated stent. It would last a lot longer than the uncoated stent.

With that diagnosis, I waited over a month and was obviously concerned. Although, I experienced no pain or discomfort, I was still anxious. One day, I did experience pain in my chest and difficulty in breathing and asked Lin to drive me to the Heart Hospital emergency room.

I was admitted and again they performed an angiogram. The physician told me that he now had the coated stents available and said he could put one in. He added that, while they were now available, the coated stent that he had, would have to be administered under a double blind protocol; meaning that I might get the coated stent, or an uncoated stent and he and I would have no idea which one would be used. I quickly said, "No thanks; I don't want a Band-Aid, I want it fixed. So, I think I will have the bypass." Although, this doctor did the stents and not the bypass operations, he said, "That's what I'd do."

The next day, they wheeled me down into the operating room area and a prep-nurse asked me. "Do you play the violin?"

"No, why do you ask?"

"Because we would like to take your radial artery instead of your saphenous vein as one of the bypass vessels. If you played the violin, then you might suffer some reduction in your playing ability. If you don't play the violin, you will notice nothing different."

"I would prefer that you take the radial artery. It makes much more sense. The vein has valves, a thin wall, not capable for expansion and relaxation. Please do it."

My recovery was fairly rapid, but not much fun. Because they did not take my leg vein (saphenous vein), there was no leg pain, which others have said was more painful than the chest wall recovery. One curious aspect was the following. Apparently they had given me some sort of narcotic (codeine I think). As I was looking at the ceiling and closed my eyes, I started to see an exact replica of a famous poster of Che Guevera's face. I told them to stop giving me those pain pills, whatever they were. Then the image disappeared.

I have to say, in all honesty, that I know that I am not the smartest person in the world and do not always make the best decisions. When Lin and Colin and I moved to ABQ, I promised to Lin to break my relationship to Marta and stay with my family.

However, with this life or death experience, I thought to myself that I should be completely honest and decide what did I want from the rest of my life. For the following reasons, I was not happy in my marriage. Lin was a very nice person, but we had many area of definite conflict. She spent too much money. She thought I was a miser. I was optimistic, she was pessimistic. I was a neat freak, she was a clutter girl. She liked to eat out, I did not. I was friendly, she was not. I liked sex, she did not. I paid off her excessive credit card bills three times. Each time she said, she would never do it again. Each time the debt paid off amounted into the thousands of dollars, which did not please me at all.

With Marta, at the time, there were no conflicts in those categories and there was a spark and chemistry that still prevails today (20/7/2018), years later. I made a list of comparisons of advantages and disadvantages and there was no contest. So, I decided to continue my association with Marta because I could not get her out of my mind and had such a high regard for her personal ethics.

I BUY MY SECOND AIRPLANE

Even though I thoroughly enjoyed flying the powered parachute, I wanted to start flying a fixed wing plane again and preferably a tail dragger, as they looked to be a lot of fun. So, while cruising through the internet, I came upon an experimental aircraft called the Rans Coyote II. I said, "Hey, Colin, look at this."

He came over, looked at the web site for a couple of minutes and said, "That looks great dad, go ahead and buy it."

So I called the guy back in North Carolina and told him that I was interested. We tentatively agreed upon a price and then I thought before I conclude the deal, I should investigate other planes for sale at the Sun and Fun EAA (Experimental Airplane Association) Meeting in Florida that would take place in a couple of weeks.

After driving down to Florida, visiting and staying with relatives along the way, I decided to buy the Rans Coyote II in North Carolina. I stayed with my cousin Barney Stewart and a good buddy of mine, Bill Sutton in the Charlotte area.

I guess one (or two) could say that sometimes I am impetuous and naïve. After I bought the plane for $39,000, I went up with a flight instructor, who painfully explained to me that I could not fly that plane until I had at least 25 hours of instruction on how to handle a tail dragger, or a rear wheeled plane as some called that type.

I called John Lorenz, one of my Civil Air Patrol (CAP) buddies and he agreed to fly back to Charlotte and fly the plane back to ABQ and then train me in becoming proficient in it. Unfortunately, he miscalculated and ran out of gas about a mile from the runway in Amarillo, where he intended to refuel. This caused a delay involving the FAA and local investigations into the mishap.

Eventually, John gave me the training I needed and soon, I was soloing all around New Mexico. My last lesson was almost a disaster. John said, "Meet me at the airport around 4 pm and we can get the cross wind segment in. This is the only training that you lack."
So, I met him at the airport and he walked up and said, "Stew, just fly around by yourself because as you can see there is no cross wind at all."

I said, "Okay." And I took off to go joy riding around the mountains in the area. After about three quarters of an hour, I noticed some very dark clouds developing to the west and north. I thought, 'Perhaps it would be prudent for me to head back to the airport.' When I tried to land, I just could not line up with the landing strip because the cross wind from the south was so strong.

The runway at Edgewood air park where I trained, was more narrow than a one way roadway. After the second unsuccessful attempt to land, I called John on the radio and told him my plight. Unfortunately, the radio kept cutting out and it was very difficult to hear him or for him to hear me. His house was right next to the runway, so he could actually see that I was having trouble landing. I think that he was telling me to fly to Moriarty and land there since that airport had a much wider and longer runway.

After the third attempt, I headed for Moriarty. A cross wind landing was also necessary there as well. The wind was directly from the south and it made no difference whether I landed due east or due west. Since I was coming from the west, I chose to land straight toward the east. Instead of crabbing into the wind, I dipped my wing into the wind and had to raise it as I almost touched down on the runway. As soon as I touched down I immediately had to hold the control stick hard to the right to prevent from being blown over. Luckily everything went smoothly. I had to be very careful with the controls whenever I turned and adjust the controls again as I taxied around.

I could not stop the plane and get out, because the wind would have twisted the plane's orientation and sent it on his way, so I had to remain in the plane and wait for John to appear. He arrived about 10 minutes later and we had a great deal of trouble tying the plane down, but we were eventually successful. Later on I heard that the wind around the time that I landed was 31 knots. My Rans Coyote II is only cleared to land and take off in a cross wind below 18 knots. All is well that ends well, and I thank my lucky stars everything turned out okay.

2002

I MOVED TO ANOTHER HOUSE

After long consideration following different conflicts at home I decided to move out of the house. Rather than renting an apartment somewhere, I settled on buying a small house. I looked in the newspaper, saw a house for sale not too far away and Colin and I went to look at it.

The house had a new hot water heater, a new stove and refrigerator and new carpeting. They were asking $122,000 for it. I offered $118, 000. The seller said, "I've already got an offer of $119, 000 for it." I countered, "I'll give you $122,000 cash for it right now." He said okay.

Since I knew precious little about real estate, I called the real estate sales woman that sold our first house to us in ABQ. I told her I would give her $150 if she would meet me and the present owners and go over the deal. She agreed and I'm so glad she did. At the meeting she insisted that an inspection be done and everything agreed to before the sale. Several items were corrected and a warranty deed issued that became invaluable later on after the sale. Without her help I would have been out of luck.

Colin and my neighbor helped me move. Unbeknownst to me at that time, I was lucky enough to have moved next door to the best neighbor I have ever had. Josh Stewart ended up being my philosophical companion (we had stimulating discussions); he mowed my very small yard (because he had a very small yard), he watered, aerated and fertilized my yard when I was gone visiting Marta. He drove me to the airport, even at 5 am. Unfortunately, he moved away after a while and I still miss him today.

MY SON PHIL MOVES BACK TO AUSTRALIA

My son's wife, Donna, had kicked him out of the house in Southern California. She did this not because of infidelity, but because he was going bankrupt and did not want to get a job for various reason. So, he fabricated this scheme, saying that god told him to go to Australia and windsurf around the continent for world peace.

He had never been windsurfing in his life, but was angry that no one on either side of the Pacific would loan him money for his project. Talking to him was like talking to a brick wall. Nothing would dissuade him. I ended up paying substantial sums to the divorce and bankruptcy lawyers left behind in the wake of his departure.

2003

COLIN GOES TO RANGER SCHOOL

Colin and I both joined the Civil Air Patrol (CAP) when we first came to ABQ and both of us enjoyed it very much. When Colin was 14 years old he qualified and applied to the CAP ranger school. It took place in the mountains of southern Pennsylvania.

We loaded up the Shasta Cheyenne RV, that looked like a bread truck, as there were no insignias or markings of any kind. We took Shotgun the dog and towed a 2002 Saturn behind it. At some of the RV parks in which we would stop overnight some of the other RVers would ask me why I didn't have any markings on our RV. Sometimes, just for fun, I would tell them that we were part of the witness protection program and we had Jimmy Hoffa in our RV, moving around constantly. Hardly anyone believed me I am sure.

Along the way, we stopped to visit my high school buddy Charles Schweinle and his wife Sally. They invited us both to stay inside their house overnight. It was really hot in Arkansas and they had air conditioning, so I took them up on their offer. Colin opted to stay in the RV with Shotgun.

During the night there was a very strong thunderstorm. Colin usually slept in the bunk bed above the driver's cab, but because I wasn't there, he slept in my bed back in the bedroom. He had opened the vent above the bed. When the rain came and rained onto him in the middle of the night, he just got up and went to the bed above the driver's cab. He never bothered to close the vent. Consequently, the whole bed covers and mattress were completely soaked. We had to take the mattress out and put it on Schweinle's driveway to dry it out. I'm sure his neighbors were impressed with the hicks that were staying with him.

We stopped along the way to see another high school buddy, Bernie Hodge and his wife, Martha, in Ozark, Missouri and made our way to Hawk Mountain Sanctuary in Pennsylvania where the ranger camp was. While Colin was at the ten day camp, I visited some of my Johns Hopkins buddies in Philadelphia, Baltimore and Washington, D.C. Also, I stayed in the RV near my ex-wife's house in Baltimore and saw my father's last wife in Washington, D.C.

When I went to the graduation ceremony at the Ranger camp, it was a wet rainy mess. At the conclusion of the camp as we were packing up the car (the RV probably wouldn't have made it up the mountain roads), Colin began to just cry like a baby; uncontrollable sobs. I thought to myself, 'What have I done to my poor son? What have I put him through that was so terrible?' As Colin started to regain his composure and still sniffling, he said, "I loved it dad. I just loved it."

There was a problem which he had to overcome. When we were preparing for the camp, Colin wanted to buy MRE's (Meals Ready to Eat). You could buy them at an army surplus stores, but they were about $3.00 each. We had to take with us his entire food supply; that was for about 20 some meals. Being the fugal person (read cheapskate) I am, I talked him into buying Chef Boyardee cans of spaghetti that were on sale for 99 cents each. The MRE's would have been much lighter to carry. Therefore when they went out on patrol, he had to lug the heavy cans around with him.

On the way back to ABQ, Colin attended another CAP camp at an army base just south of Indianapolis, Indiana. While he was at the weeklong camp, I stayed with my college roommate, Page Faulk and his wife Klara in Indianapolis. I had parked my RV in a parking lot just across from their condo. The president of the upscale condo complex told Page, that it was not possible to have RV's parked in the complex's parking lot. Page told her that I had just dropped off my son at the deployment camp for Afghanistan and I would be leaving soon. When she heard this explanation, she said, "Oh, in that case, tell him he can leave the RV in the lot as long as he wants."

2004

CRASHED MY PLANE

Wayne Brewer, a fellow powered parachute pilot, and I were going to fly over the Canadian river valley to see about enticing the other PPG (Powered Para-Gliders) club members to go there on a weekend. He and I had both checked with the FAA flight Service advisor where we heard independently that there would be no significant surface winds at Las Vegas, NM where we would have to refuel.

I picked him up at his home and we were airborne by 8:30 am from my home base of Belen, NM about 45 miles south of ABQ. After clearing the Manzano Mountains, I let him fly as I wanted to become better acquainted with the operating features of my new GPS. After a routine landing at Las Vegas, New Mexico, we topped off the gas tanks and resumed our journey toward the Canadian river valley. About half way there, Wayne complained of nausea, which was so intense that he asked to return as soon as possible to Las Vegas. The air was smooth, but the gas fumes had got to him.

I gave him my Nature Conservancy cloth bag and told him to use it if he just had to barf. I was giving him a countdown as we flew rapidly back toward Las Vegas.

"Wayne, we're only 23 miles from Las Vegas."

"Wayne, we're 16 miles away."

"Wayne, we're - - -." I never got to finish my sentence. He barfed into the bag. An ugly sickly smell enveloped the cock pit and I didn't feel so shiny myself.

When we landed, Wayne went immediately to the bathroom to wash his face. When he returned he said that he had to lie down. So for an hour or so, he continually declined to get into the air plane to go back to ABQ. I read magazines and talked with the airport manager. I was a little anxious to leave, because, I knew that in New Mexico, the winds do some squirrelly things in the afternoon. Even though the flight service advisor had assured us that there would be no significant surface winds, I wanted to get back to Belen before night fall for sure.

Around 2:30 pm we decided to leave. I looked at the weather notice and saw that there were cross winds at 8 knots, gusting to 12. So I was mentally prepared to handle them on takeoff. I taxied into position and gradually increased the throttle. As we lifted off and were climbing, suddenly a very strong wind rotated my plane to the left. I immediately corrected by jamming the control stick to the right, which (thank God) leveled the plane and then the next instance we hit the ground extremely hard.

As I said loudly, "What happened?" Wayne, was out the door and trotting away from the plane. I sat there briefly in a daze. My neck hurt with a sharp pain at the base of my skull. I also exited the plane very rapidly.

Surveying the damage, I saw that both landing gears had collapsed and the propeller was twister. Everything else was intact that I could determine. Unknown to me at the time the, ELT (Emergency Locator Transmitter) had been activated and the FAA was aware of the crash. We walked across the field to the pilot's lounge and I called the FAA to inform them of the accident. They said that they would send out an investigator within a couple of hours and for us to remain there until he arrived.

While we were waiting, I saw what had happened. For the next three hours, I saw (and so did Wayne) at least three dust devils move across the field. They were mesocyclones, meaning that they were much wider than the usual dust devils and there was no dust. It had rained a few days before and the desert ground was still damp. We could detect these mega-dust devils by the fact that there were many tumble weeds sucked up into the vortex and you could clearly see the width and vigor of the wind revealed.

I got a call from the FAA and they asked me to go out and deactivate the ELT. I walked to the plane and reached back and thought that I turned it off. I could not see it, but flipped the switch. Then I looked at the throttle and noticed that it was not at the full throttle position, but was at half throttle. I strongly suspect that I caused the crash. In the shock of the unexpected rotation of the plane, apparently I pulled back on the throttle and lost lift. There is a slim possibility that I may have moved the throttle after the crash, but I doubt that.

There was no insurance involved, as I just had liability insurance in case I crashed on someone else's property. I called Randy, the owner of the Rans airplane company and told him if he came and got the plane he could have it for $5,000. I took pictures of the plane with my digital camera and sent them to him. He agreed to buy it, so it wasn't a complete loss (just close to it).

Wayne, was a private investigator and he called his assistant who drove up and picked us up and took us back to Belen to get my car. Wayne was not injured at all. My doctor after twisting my head in every direction said that I was okay also. Interestingly, every time I turn my head after this episode, I hear a crunching sound, but no problem what so ever (except for this occasional catch in my neck associated with this sound).

I STOP FLYING THE POWERED PARACHUTE

A week after I crashed my plane I went to see Marta in Slovakia. She asked me to stop flying. I told her, you don't have to ask, as I had decided to stop flying planes anyway. When I went to the flight service station to hand in my report of the crash, the FAA official said, to me, "When do you want me to give you your check ride, so you can start flying again?"

"Never," was my immediate reply.

She said, "You don't mean that because if you don't have a check ride, you have to hand in your pilot's license and you can never fly again."

I responded, "That's fine with me and that's why I said never."

She added, "Well, you just think about it for a while. You may change your mind. Most pilots do. Others have changed their mind and you'd be sorry if you hand in your license, because you will have to go all the way through flight training to get a new one. Did you ever fall of off a horse and get back on later?"

"Yes, as a matter of fact I did fall off of a horse. But that was when I was 14. I'm 67 now and believe me I do not want to fly again at this stage of my tender life."

When I got back from Slovakia, I continued to fly the powered parachute. I had crashed it a couple of times during my training and always without any injury. So, I thought that the powered parachute was innocuous and safe. This attitude was unexpectedly obliterated by a near incident that occurred on the balloon fiesta field at ABQ a few weeks after I returned from Slovakia.

Our group had been given permission to fly off of the balloon fiesta park field one week end. Most of the members of our group were already air borne when I took off from midfield. Everything seemed normal in my preflight run up and examination. As I got airborne, however, I noticed that the unit was just not climbing as fast as I expected. On my right there were two hot air balloons that had just lifted off and several to the right of them which were inflated but still on the ground. Straight ahead, there was this large embankment just north of the field. I thought, I am going to have no choice, but to go to the left and out over a drainage canal bordering the balloon fiesta park.

Having made this necessary decision to continue to exit, I then saw the flag poles looming, which were higher than I thought to be able to go over. As luck would have it, there was just enough space between two flag poles for me to squeak through, which is exactly what I did.

My feeling of fun for the day had ended and I landed immediately and decided to stop flying for good. I never looked back on that decision. Flying was a great and an exciting hobby, but not a necessity at my age. I loved it and am so glad that I did it, but my reflexes and other sensory modalities had reached the retirement age.

Marta was happy and I was happy that she was happy.

2005

LIN FILES FOR DIVORCE

Lin told me that she was going to file for divorce. I said, "Okey-dokey." She asked who was going to be my lawyer and I said, "I don't want one." She said, that her lawyer said that I should have one, but still I respectfully disagreed and did not get a lawyer. I read some of the relevant rules and regulations about divorce in New Mexico to my satisfaction.

Everybody said that I was crazy not to get a lawyer. My explanation was that I thought I would be better off without a lawyer for the following reasons. I have heard that often times the respective lawyers sometimes get together and work things so, they can induce confrontation and dissention if there is none, in order to drag out the process and create a more lucrative flow of consultation fees. I reasoned, if I objected too much, it would just mean more lawyer time and create more problems than were already there.

One of my high school buddies told me that my attitude, of just accepting what was offered to me would not be fair to Marta. I took his advice to heart, and paid more attention to the details of the process. The day before I was to leave to go to Slovakia, I went down to the lawyer's office to sign the divorce papers.

There was one sentence that bothered me a great deal. It said very clearly that if I ever became late with either the alimony or child support payments, that I would be liable for unspecified interest payments. I just said, unless that sentence was omitted, I would not sign the agreement. So, I just drew a line though it and initialed it. It was taken out. I thought that the settlement was unfair. Lin thought that the settlement was unfair. I am sure there could have been more give and take on both sides, but I was just happy the ordeal was over.

2006

MARTA AND I BUY A NEW CAR IN SLOVAKIA

Marta bought a Daewoo Tico car back in 1996. We drove it all over, but not on long overnight trips. We were going to go to a time share in Austria in September and the reliance of the Tico for such a long journey was under some slight suspicion. So I agreed to pay for half and Marta paid for half of a Fiat Panda that we had seen roaming around town.

We went to the Fiat dealer that we knew about and decided to buy a slightly larger, more heavy and suitable car for long distances. It was a Punto. As I remember the sequence of events, every process of the purchase was cumbersome and filled with steps I still cannot understand, compared to my experiences in the United States.

We decided to buy the car. But we could not get the car until we had gone to the bank and deposited the money directly into their account; which we did the next day. But we still could not pick up the car, until certain checks had been dealt with which showed that we actually had deposited the money.

A couple of days later we picked up the car. We were told that we had to have the car "inspected". I said to Marta, "Why do we have to have a brand new car inspected?"

She said, "They want to check the engine number."

"It's a new car"

"Well, it has to be done."

"How do we do it?"

"Well, we go to the inspection station?"

"Where is that?"

186

"I don't know. I'll have to find out."

So, after investigating the whereabouts of the inspection station, we headed out to find it. It was not easy. There were no signs and the directions given were very vague. We get to the general area and see this deserted parking lot, which is difficult to reach by the existing visible roads. Wandering around an empty flea market, we eventually figured out how to reach the huge empty parking lot. There were no signs, just a lone car with a man smoking a cigarette.

We pulled up next to him and asked where was the inspection station. He said, he would inspect the car. The inspection consisted of him looking briefly under the hood and then examining the serial numbers on the inside of the door.

I said to Marta, "Hooray, now we have a new car."

"Not so fast. We still have to register it and get the license tag."

"Where do we do that?"

"At the police station."

So we went downtown to the police station. We waited in one line for quite some time. When we got to the head of the line, we were told that we were in the wrong line and had to go to another part of the building. There was another long line, which we dutifully waited in for another long time period. Marta then was issued a chit. With the chit, we had to go to another line in the same building to pay the registration fee. With the registration fee paid, we went back to the very first long line that we were in to begin with and got the necessary papers. The whole process was not easy and seemed unnecessarily cumbersome and inefficient.

2007

BY A MIRACLE COLIN GRADUATES FROM THE FLORIDA AIR ACADEMY

It pains me to this day to talk about it. Colin hates math. He has flunked it many times. Actually, he hates school. In an attempt to get him through high school, he attended several schools; Menaul school (high school prep), La Cueva high school, Amy Behl Charter school, New Mexico Military Academy summer school and finally Florida Air Academy.

Florida Air Academy is a boarding and private day school in Melbourne, Florida. There is a large contingent of international students from wealthy people from all over the world. It is very expensive. The only reason that we could afford to send Colin there was the desperation he caused us in ABQ; the fear that he was never going to pass math; the agonizing fights to get him to do his homework; and a myriad of other relevant reasons. Primarily, we used the money from my mother's trust fund to pay for his board and tuition, which had been earmarked for college (a word which was devoid of meaning with regard to Colin's future at the time.)

I arrived Thursday evening and checked into a nice motel (Marriott). I honestly did not know whether or not Colin was going to graduate. I went to talk with the commandant and asked what was his chance to graduate. He replied that he was sure that Colin would graduate. When I asked about math, he said that he had passed.

The way I understand it, as it was explained to me, is the following. Even though Colin got a 38 on one test, since it was flunking, at the end of the course, they changed it to the demarcation for an "F" which was 55. So that the actual grade was changed to the 55 so he could end up passing.

All of this was well and good (I thought). As it turned out, Colin happened to have done particularly well in the eyes of the military aspect of the training at Florida Air Academy. On an earlier trip to visit his school, he had received an award for outstanding contribution to the ROTC equivalent program. Soo, he was in charge of the big parade in front of the whole school to impress the hundreds of parents there for graduation.

So, all was well and good I thought. At the very end of the parade, Colin addressed the crowd with his parting remarks. I listened to him

188

with pride. After the parade, everybody went to the gymnasium for the award ceremony and a dinner. I looked for Colin. I could not see him anywhere. All of sudden, one of his best friends came up to me and said, "Mr. Odendhal, I think you should know that Colin has been band from participation in this event."

"Why on earth is that and where is he?

"The president is mad at his remarks at the parade and has sent him to the back room of the quartermaster's room."

"What did he say that pissed off the president?"

"I can't say. Maybe you'd better go there and talk to him."

So, I went there after I told my ex-wife Lin about this unfortunate development. Colin and another cadet were just sitting in the back room of the operations office. He was obviously upset. I said to him, "Why are you here?"

He said, "I said something at the parade that pissed off the president."

"What did you say?"

"Well, in my farewell speech I can mention one of the other cadets that I admire. So, I mentioned this guy that is not going to be able to graduate."

"Why did you mention that guy?"

"Because, I felt that he got a bum deal."

"Well you really shouldn't have done that apparently. Are you going to be able to attend the graduation ceremony tomorrow?"

"I don't know", was his response.

"I'll go talk with the president and see what he says."

Then I turned to the other cadet and asked, "Why are you in here and what did you do or not do?"

The other cadet said, "I didn't do anything wrong. They just put me in here for safe keeping."

Astonished at his reply, I asked, "Why would they do that?"

He said, "Because my dad has custody after the divorce and there is an injunction for my mother not to see me here."

I said, "Gosh, I'm sorry to hear about your troubles."

I then left and went back to the gym where the festivities were in full swing. I walked up to one of the school officials and said, "Where is the president? I'd like to talk with him."

The official replied, "He is going to make the opening address in a few minutes and perhaps you can talk with him after that."

I searched for Lin and her friends and went to sit next to them and explained to Lin more about what Colin had said. It was hard to talk because of the back ground noise and we resigned ourselves to keep quiet and listen to the presentations from the podium. After the president had concluded his talk he walked off of the stage and was headed for the door. Quick as greased lightning, I intercepted him just as he reached the door.

I said, "I'm Colin Odend'hal's father and I would like to talk to you."

He quickly side-stepped me and said, "I'm sorry, I can't talk to you right now." And out the door he fled. Bewildered, I turned to another school official standing next to the door and asked, "What's going on here?"

The school official said, "He's got some big problems that demand his attention right now."

I thought to myself, 'I hope his big problem is not Colin', and returned to the table. After about 20 minutes, I saw the president coming back through the door and once again, I intercepted him as he headed for the podium.

"Why did you stop my son from attending these festivities?" I asked politely.

"Because he insulted me", was his vigorous response.

I countered, "I'll bet 99.9 % of those in attendance had no idea of what Colin said, or the implications."

"I knew", he hollered, "and I didn't like it a bit."

"I see you point", I interjected, and asked meekly, "Will you let him attend graduation tomorrow?"

"I haven't made up my mind on that matter. I'll go talk to him after the ceremony." With that, he didn't excuse himself, but left me standing surprised as he marched off back toward the stage.

After the ceremony as we walked out with everyone else, we saw two police cars in the front of the school. Lin and her sister both gasped and said, "My god they are taking him away." I said, "I really don't think they are here because of Colin."

My suspicion turned out to be correct. The police were called because the other young man in suspension was the concern. His mother had been seen on the premises and there was a court order for her not to appear. So, the cops were there to escort her off of the school grounds.

Anyway, not to prolong the climax of the event, Colin did attend graduation and successfully received his ill-deserved high school diploma. He was so happy and relieved, that once again as he had displayed at the ranger camp, he cried like a baby. So, $60,000.00 down the drain, burped up one sheet of paper with the union card printed in my blood, sweat and tears.

Years later Colin told me, "You know, dad, did I ever tell you how Bell (one of his best friends) and I passed math our senior year?"

"I don't think you ever addressed that issue with me before."

"Well, we were not terribly attentive and Bell even slept though some of the tests. He actually put his head down on the desk and went to sleep. We were always joking around and irritating the teacher. Toward the end of the year, Bell and I went up to her and said that we were looking forward to next year when we would probably be back to take her math course again. She looked horrified at this prospect. So that's how we passed the course."

2008

YEAR OF THE TIME SHARES

Briefly, Marta and I wrote a grant to travel to the Caribbean to visit three private veterinary schools to investigate the possible collaboration with the veterinary school in Kosice in Slovakia. On the way back, we rented a car in Atlanta and drove to the Loreley Resort in Helen , Georgia. This is my home time share and we enjoyed the week very much before we flew back to Slovakia the first week in June.

In August, Marta, her sister Ludmila and I drove to Meribel, France to another time share in the Alps. We enjoyed beautiful hiking trails and luckily had good weather. The three day drive became a little exhausting, however.

Returning back to the United States we rested for a few weeks in ABQ and then took the RV and Jeep and went to a time share in Corpus Christi, Texas. The time share was right on the inter-coastal waterway and it was marvelous to see the water birds and other sea creatures. There were grunions, that many call a trash fish that continually jumped out of the water. We went to a small fishing village and saw porpoises when we took the ferry across the inlet to Corpus Christi bay. Then at a sanctuary, I saw the biggest crabs I have ever seen and roseate spoonbills and a myriad of other sea birds.

We stopped outside of San Antonio and visited my friend Krishna Murthy. He took us to an Indian restaurant for lunch and then to the Riverwalk and the Alamo.

For thanksgiving, we shared a time share with my ex-daughter-in-law, Donna and her husband, Gregg and my two grandkids, Weston and Abby in Las Vegas, Nevada. One day we took the kids to the Grand Canyon and another day to the tower which overlooks Las Vegas. So it was the year of the time shares.

2009

BOUGHT COLIN A MOBILE HOME

With the cessation of alimony payments to my ex-wife, she said she couldn't afford to feed and clothe Colin and that he should move in with Marta and me. She also wanted Colin to pay her back the money that she had spent for his telephone, insurance and other incidental expenses over the past few years.

Marta and I, fearing a loss of our privacy and other complications, decided to find him a place nearby. So we found him a nice one bedroom apartment not too far away. He qualified based on his income from his job (as a security guard) and Marine reserve pay, so I did not have to sign as a responsible parent. However, when we got back from Slovakia, he had been suspended from his job as a night watchman because he went to sleep. He was caught, and admitted it with no excuses. They were so pleased with him not arguing about that they hired him back.

Unfortunately, he could not pay his rent for that month. I paid it and thought my goodness, this could be a problem later on, if I wasn't in town. So one day returning from the Sandia Casino where we enjoyed a senior discount lunch occasionally, usually with our neighbor Jake Bordenave, Marta saw a sign at this mobile home park. The sign said, "Homes from $15,000".

We enquired at the mobile home park and found out that they had sold the $15,000 mobile home and only had a few others for sale, but they were in the $30,000 to $40,000 category. Thus, we then began to read the newspapers and internet looking for reasonably priced mobile homes.

There was a 14 by 70 foot mobile home for sale on Craig's list in a mobile home park on the west side of ABQ. Marta and I went to look at it and later brought Colin out to see it. We all liked it and we liked the lady that owned it as well. She asked $11,000, but when we said we did not want the shed, she dropped the price to $10,000. So we bought it.

The trouble was that the mobile home park was not very nice and it was so far from where Marta and I lived. We found a much nicer mobile home park only 2 miles from our house. It was much nicer because it was much more expensive and had very rigid requirements. The rental space was $411 per month compared to $350 per month where the mobile home was then located. However they had a special attractive offer for those who moved into the park. The rent would be frozen at $199 per month for two years, if you moved in a new or late model used mobile home which was approved by the home office in California. We submitted photos of Colin's mobile home and it was approved with the stipulation that the trim needed to be toned down because it was too bright.

Part of the requirements for newly introduced mobile homes was that they had to have: a new deck built for each door; an irrigation system installed; ground cover to prevent weeds; xeriscaped with rocks throughout the rest of the lot; and at least ten plants. Even though we still liked the mobile home after we found out that it was only 52 feet long instead of the 70 feet advertised; we needed a lot more rocks that we had originally calculated to cover the lot.

The total cost of moving the mobile home to the new park exceeded half of the cost to buy the mobile home in the first place. But it was worth it. Colin was in a much nicer mobile home park, he was much closer and the monthly cost would be much lower for him for the first two years. Then as the owner of the mobile home, I felt it was unlikely that I would ever evict him. So I felt that he was secure for now (Hooray).

ROAD ACCIDENT IN SLOVAKIA

When we went back to Slovakia, I met a nice mixed couple (American male and Slovak female) at the Info-USA office in Kosice. They were from Presov, a city about 25 miles north of Kosice, but they were about the same age as Marta and me. We enjoyed each other's company and made several trips around Slovakia together. One week end we drove to the high Tatra Mountains for a hike.

Jim and Tatiana took their car (a recent model Volvo sedan). Marta's sister, Ludmila went with us. Tatiana drove, as Jim did not have his Slovak driver's license yet. Tatiana is a good driver. She is cautious and does not drive too fast. On the way back from our hike, it was raining quite heavily near the mountains, but cleared up the farther we got away from the mountains.

We were driving through a medium sized town, the rain had diminished, but we were approaching a slight curve in the road. A young man came around the curve, perhaps a little faster than he should have, given the wet pavement and he skidded and then lost control of his small car. Tatiana saw this and tried to turn to the right to avoid him, but his car slammed into the left front fender and spun us around and into the oncoming traffic, which luckily had stopped.

Marta was thrown against the door and the handle struck her rib cage. She also had a gash on her knee. Ludmila's head hit the door window. Everyone else was without injury. Marta was taken to the local hospital and given an x-ray. She had no broken bones. Both cars were totaled. The young man driving the other car was okay.

It is amazing that you can be doing nothing wrong and in a split second your whole life can change forever. Luckily, as far as we know, everything turned out okay, so far (two days after the accident).

EPILOGUE

2010 – After a decade of trying to make Marta feel at home in ABQ and she trying to make me more satisfied with her home town of Kosice in Slovakia, we agreed to a compromise by moving to Athens, GA. This would reduce our travel time between Slovakia and America. It would also bring us closer to my son, Colin, who had moved to Florida the year before. We arrived in Athens in the nick of time before a tremendous snow and ice storm hit. Unfortunately, the movers did not arrive until a week later. Both of our backs were aching from a week of sleeping on the hard wood floor.

2011 – Early in the year, Colin was fired from his job as a security officer in Florida for being late to work. He was late because of a stuck draw bridge he says. He moved back to live with his mother in ABQ. In September about two days after we had just returned to America, Marta got a phone call from her sister that their mother was in the hospital. Marta rushed back to Kosice for a double tragedy. Her mother died in December at the age of 87 and three weeks later her sister died from an embolism following cancer surgery at 65.

2012 – When Colin graduated from high school, he was worthless as a mature academician. Even though he was accepted at Georgia College in Milledgeville, GA, I refused to pay for him to go to college anywhere in the universe. He was gainfully employed in ABQ, but I invited him to come to Georgia and live with us and go to a local community college.

The strain on all of us with him addicted to video games in the middle of the night was agonizing. I bought a condo just around the block for him to live in. To my astonishment he made straight A grades at Gainesville State College his first semester.

Marta and I got married March 13, 2012 in Athens that made our life and travelling much easier. When we first obtained Marta's visa to come to the United States we were told by the embassy personnel in Bratislava, Slovakia that she could stay for up to 6 months, go out for a brief period of time, and return for 6 months. However, the immigration folks in the U.S. said that was not true. She could only stay in the USA for one 6 month period out of a year. There were other irritating conditions changed by the immigration folks later on as well that we felt were unnecessarily restrictive for retired people.

When we called them on the phone, some recording eventually answered, and we were finally successful in negotiating the options to connect to the correct party, and asked them a question, and got an answer, we were ecstatic. The trouble was, when we called the next week and asked the same question, to confirm the answer, often times, we got a different answer.

2013 – Marta's daughter and her husband moved to Prague in the neighboring Czech Republic. We visited them several times and fell in love with that city for a myriad of reasons. Colin did a summer semester abroad in University College of London.

2014 – I told Marta that I would not mind living in Prague, as we were getting older and her daughter was a physician who would be useful as we started to fall apart. Marta speaks Slovak, which the Czechs understand. Their language is so similar that Marta can understand Czech with very little trouble. Colin transferred to the University of Georgia (UGA) and majored in international relations.

2015 – We bought a small apartment in Prague, not too far from where her daughter lived. Unfortunately, the very week after we moved in, Marta's daughter came to our apartment for lunch and informed us that she had taken a new job in Munich, Germany. She moved there the next month. I applied for temporary residency status in the Czech Republic, but had to leave before it could be completed. Colin went to China for study during the Maymester accelerated semester. He absolutely loved the experience.

2016 – Marta's daughter took a new job in Mannheim, Germany. We moved stuff from Kosice, Slovakia to Praha (that is the local name in Czech for Prague [which is the English name for Praha; the Germans call it Prag]). In July I finally received my temporary resident permit for the Czech Republic. In August Colin graduated from the University of Georgia with a double major of International Relations and Political Science.

2017 – The high light of 2017 was the 10 day tour that Marta and I took to Costa Rica in the spring. The smoking volcanos, lush vegetation and the diversity of the animals were amazing. Tragedy struck just before Christmas on December 14th, as my son, Philip died in Australia from an over dose of heroin. For Christmas we took Colin for a short visit to New Orleans and spent Christmas day with him in Hattiesburg, Mississippi where he was working as the assistant director of Dismas Charities.

2018 - Marta and I spent most of the spring trying to arrange health insurance, as we were notified on December 28, 2017 that we would have no health insurance effective after December 31, 2017. A night-mare of misinformation, conflicting responses from multiple sources, and confusing government regulations followed. The good news was that my book *Why I am A Happy Agnostic* was published and I saw my grandkids and their mother at the California Polytechnic State University in San Luis Obispo, California in March.

POST SCRIPT

When I started writing on this book in 2009, my original intention was to learn touch typing and fight boredom. But as it progressed I thought that I would complete it and give it to my grandchildren when I finished. However, after I had written about my teenage years it dawned upon me that it would not be a good idea if they should try to emulate my spirited and dangerous behavior in their teenage years. So any thought of publication as a book was not considered. Now that they are both over 20 years old and obviously have more common sense than I ever had, I have decided to share my whole life story with whoever.

My grandfather, Charles Joseph Odend'hal, Sr. (Purtsie) wrote his autobiography when he was 95 years old. My sister gave him an empty paged book for his birthday and he wrote the whole book in pencil and then copied over each letter with a ball point pen. I found out that he had spent a great deal of time in and around the Pribilof Islands in the Bering Sea of Alaska in 1911 protecting the Northern Fur Seals from the pelagic harvesting of their pelts when he was in the U. S. Coast Guard. I was there the summer of 1966 (over a half of a century afterwards) with the U.S. Fish and Wildlife Service investigating the causes of death of the Northern Fur Seal pups.

Two other very short stories about my grandfather. When he was 94 years old he had a minor accident and we decided to take the car keys away so he would not endanger himself and others around him. When I picked him up to take him over to our Christmas party, he said, "I don't know why they took the keys to my car away, because the only driving that I did was to go to the liquor store." On Purtsie's 100th birthday, my brother-in-law gave him a "life-time membership" in his VFW (Veterans of Foreign Wars) Club.

Just before my father, Capt. Charles Joseph Odend'hal, Jr. USN Ret. died in 1983 at the age of 71, we had a conversation about the treatment that he received at the Naval Hospital in Bethesda, Maryland. He suffered from metastatic colon cancer. To treat his liver the doctors had placed a catheter into his hepatic artery to more adequately infuse his liver with a higher level of a chemotherapeutic cocktail.

Unfortunately for my dad, the catheter pulled out of the hepatic artery and flopped around the lumen of the aorta until the tip of the catheter buried itself in the muscular aortic wall and caused indescribable pain to which he was subjected.

I said to him, "I do not like the fact they the doctors there are just using you as a guinea pig."

He said to me, "I don't mind that they may be using me as a guinea pig. Despite the excruciating pain, if it results in the discovery of a new more effective treatment that helps others I can tolerate it."

ABOUT THE AUTHOR

Stewart Odendhal was born in San Diego, California (1937) and grew up in Oklahoma City, Oklahoma. He was educated at UCLA (B.A. 1960), the University of California – Davis (D.V.M. 1967) and the University of Missouri (Ph.D. 1977). He was employed primarily in research and teaching at: Johns Hopkins University's School of Hygiene and Public Health (1967 – 1971), Pfizer, Inc. (1971 – 1973), and the University of Georgia's School of Veterinary Medicine (1978 – 1998).

His diverse research interests have taken him all over the world and has resulted in scientific publications in many different fields of endeavor such as: Anatomy, Anthropology, Clinical Veterinary Medicine, Ecology, Epidemiology, Geography, Immunology, Parasitology, the Physiology of Diving Mammals, and virology. His research work has been supported by major funding agencies such as: the National Institute of Health, the National Science Foundation, the National Academy of Sciences, the National Geographic Society and many others.

Since his retirement he has served as a consultant to a scientific veterinary journal; correcting papers accepted for publication by non-native English speaking scientists. He and his wife Marta Prosbova live in Athens, GA, USA in the winter and in Prague, Czech Republic in the summer.

His email is: sodendhal505@aol.com or stewartodendhal@gmail.com

CPSIA information can be obtained
at www.ICGtesting.com
Printed in the USA
FSHW021958191218
54590FS

9 781723 594373